The Fundamental Trumpet

Fundamental Studies for the Developing Trumpeter

Randall Reyman
Professor Emeritus
Millikin University, Decatur, IL

Dedicated to my students who for thirty-seven years
entrusted their trumpet instruction to me.
Be assured that I learned as much from you
as you ever did from me.

The Fundamental Trumpet is the compilation of my favorite
exercises and etudes, devised for my students over the many years as trumpet professor at Millikin University. Included in the book are exercises I produced to address many of the basic challenges of my trumpet students.

Please feel free to copy any of these exercises for your students. I hope you will find them as useful as I did. Best of luck. RR

Find out more about me and my work at
www.randallreyman.com

Kindle Direct Publishing
ISBN: 9781794233553

To order more copies, go to:
Amazon.com

The Fundamental Trumpet
Contents

Fundamentals of Trumpet Playing and Practice	4
Exercises:	
1. The Routine	9
2. The Remedial Routine	16
3. Melodic Phrases	20
4. Joy of Breathing	22
5. Embouchure Studies (Group 1)	27
6. Embouchure Studies (Group 2)	30
7. Embouchure Studies (Group 3)	34
8. Pedal Tone Study	38
9. Single Tonguing	41
10. Multiple Tongue	46
11. Accuracy Studies	50
12. Long-setting Exercises	52
13. Tone Bending	53
14. Tuning Etudes	55
15. Fingers	56
16. Chromatics	61
17. Vibrato Study	64
18. Jazz Patterns	66
19. Playing Over Changes	68
20. Jazz Progressions	70
21. Rhythm Exercises	73
22. Major and Minor Scales	77
15 Vocalises	81
15 Rhythmical Etudes	94

Fundamentals of Trumpet Playing and Practice

Not all "fundamentals of trumpet playing" are universally accepted as fundamental. One would think that by now we would know exactly (in scientifically proven terms) how to produce the most efficient sound on the trumpet. The truth of the matter is that no scientific study has adequately measured all the variables involved in brass playing. That leaves a lot of room for divergent kinds of pedagogies, some of which can potentially confuse (and physically harm) trumpet players.

We must understand that trumpet teachers tend to base their trumpet teaching principles on their own personal experiences playing the trumpet and/or principles "revealed" to them by their teachers. These pedagogical approaches may be very successful for many of their students, but if the instruction is not based on solid natural laws and logic, the results will be far less desirable than hoped for.

I am not saying that you should question each and every thing your teacher says, but you should constantly be making assessments of the techniques you are using, and proving to yourself (over a sufficient trial period) that they are working or are not working for you. Don't just follow blindly. Constantly seek out those techniques that work best for you, asking yourself if they are logical and natural, and above all, effective. Become your own teacher!

It is interesting to note that, although the various popular trumpet pedagogies differ in many regards, they all seem to have the following two requirements in common:
1. Lips that are free (supple) to vibrate, not restricted by excessive lip tension or excessive mouthpiece pressure.
2. Airflow that is of sufficient quantity and energy to enable the lips to vibrate efficiently, energetically, and at the proper pitch.

While these may seem obvious to you, it can be helpful if you keep these general requirements in mind as you practice. By doing so, you will find that you can successfully address most playing difficulties that occur.

The Basics of Embouchure and Air

The great trumpet pedagogue Pierre Thibaud and many others believe that pedal tones help establish one's best embouchure position. After years and years of experimentation (and although you will find many trumpet teachers who may hold a differing view), I tend to agree. If you can play a full sound on a pedal F (one half step below your low F#), this should become your default embouchure setting. Once that note is established, begin working your way up with that same setting. There will be some very minor changes as you ascend, but try to keep that basic forward (slightly puckered) position as you ascend to the high register, without any attempt to press the lips together or use excessive mouthpiece pressure. This "forward" or "puckered" embouchure will accomplish two important things. First, it will offer more cushion for better endurance. Secondly, it will form an aperture that involves more lip tissue resulting in more of a
"tunnel" aperture rather than simply a small opening. This tunnel aperture will give your playing more control and comfort.

You may wonder how you can play your entire range with the same setting. The answer is with increased air speed, which is accomplished with more air compression of the lungs <u>and</u> increased tongue arch. In other words, hold the embouchure setting in place and blow faster air as you go higher. If you blow faster air but only get a louder pitch (not higher), it may be because you are allowing the increased airflow to make the aperture <u>larger</u>. Concentrate on holding the embouchure/aperture setting in place as you ascend. This will take some getting used to, and will require some time for your embouchure muscles to adapt. It may also be helpful to bring the embouchure a bit more forward as you ascend to your highest register, especially at higher volumes. Continued difficulty could also mean that you are not engaging the necessary tongue arch for that particular pitch. Keep in mind that tongue arch plays a crucial role in changing pitch on the trumpet. It will take much trial and error to find the right amount of tongue arch for all playing situations. Also be aware of the fact that the tongue can arch in various ways. The arch can be toward the front of the mouth or can be further back. I find that keeping the arch more forward is the preferable position.

It is important to realize that this approach to playing also requires a relaxed inhalation followed by an energetic exhalation. My basic approach to breathing is to take a full breath, allowing the ribcage to expand outward and upward, the shoulders to rise a bit, and the abdomen to protrude slightly. When the lungs are filled sufficiently, immediately bring the shoulders down and the abdomen muscles inward to "grip" or compress the air in the lungs. This "grip" feeling should be maintained and increased as you ascend. This is "active" blowing, as opposed to the "passive" blowing of normal "at rest" breathing. This "active" breath is quite natural, and is the same kind of blowing that one uses to blow out candles on a birthday cake or to shout or sneeze. When done correctly, the energy of the air is directed upward (not downward) through the airway, pushing the air out in a compressed (fast moving) fashion. To be clear, upon breathing, the preponderance of one's air should be collected in the chest area, not the abdominal area. Take a full breath, but not a low breath. Low breathing has often been taught as a common pedagogical technique. This counters common sense, however, since the lungs are contained in the chest area, not the abdomen. Furthermore, one never sees an athlete utilizing low breathing as he is engaged in strenuous activity. Instead, his/her chest (ribcage) moves in and out rigorously as the abdomen and diaphragm muscles work like a pump to push air out and pull air into the thoracic cavity.

Lastly, it is important to stress that while a good inhalation is critical, even more important is the quality of the exhalation. To guarantee a proper exhalation, I find it helpful to visualize the speed of the airstream being its fastest at the point of vibration (the lips). Blow to the lips. That is your target in terms of maximum air speed.

The Correct Balance

As a young trumpeter, I was very diligent in my practice. Rarely did I miss a day. Though there were many aspects of my playing that were quite deficient, I assumed that those deficiencies were simply due to the fact that my playing mechanism and associated musculature had not yet gained the necessary strength. So I continued to go through my routine everyday, wondering when this strength would be acquired. Although many trumpeters take this approach, I would like to posit an alternate approach.

My feeling is that most young or developing trumpet players are not necessarily lacking muscle strength in their playing mechanism, but rather are lacking the correct <u>balance</u> between the various aspects of trumpet playing. If there is a secret to becoming a fine trumpeter, I believe the last statement is it! Re-read it and fully consider its ramifications. Of course, embouchure strength is important. I do not mean to say that weak musculature in the embouchure is acceptable. What I am saying is that trumpet students tend to put far too much stock in muscle strength, and doing so can cause excess tension and other negative results. These students think, just as I did, that if they keep doing the same exercises the same way everyday, they will gain strength and become great trumpeters. We need to remind these students of the over-used quote often attributed to Albert Einstein which states that "repeating the same thing over and over, and expecting a different result, is one definition of insanity." Isn't this exactly what students do when they go through their exercises everyday, without thinking, hoping that the next day things will sound better?

It is important to note that when we observe close-up a really fine trumpet player in the act of playing, we don't see muscles bulging all over his/her face. On the contrary, what we see is an expression of <u>relaxed and balanced</u> control. Musculature is certainly playing a part, but primarily in terms of its balance with other aspects such as breathing efficiency, air energy, lip freedom, tongue arch, mouthpiece pressure, corner control, etc.

Therefore, I believe that students must undertake the daily task of finding that <u>balance that achieves the best result</u>. This requires much on the part of the player. It requires that the student becomes the teacher, and that the skill of acute observation is mastered. It is through constant assessment/evaluation of the various aspects mentioned above, and the student's willingness to experiment with this balance, that he/she will discover the correct balance, and become a skilled player. This is an arduous and complex process, for it requires a consistent level of concentration, and also requires the understanding that this ideal balance will vary according to register and dynamic range. This fact makes the task even more complex. This is why it must be stated here that although the player is gaining observation and analytical skill for teaching him or herself, it is most helpful if this process takes place under the watchful eye of an experienced teacher who is skillful at guiding the student. After all, doesn't it seem logical that another set of eyes and ears will be better than just one?

Now, some people may say that this approach will result in a situation described as "analysis is paralysis," and that too much analyzing gets in the way of music making. Of course this is true to the extent that one cannot go on stage to perform a piece of music while trying to analyze and control every specific aspect of one's playing. What I am talking about here is not about performance attitudes or techniques, but rather what we do in the practice room long before we walk onto the stage. If we are not willing to analyze and experiment with our playing mechanism in our practice sessions, nothing will ever change in our playing, whether it is in the practice room or on the stage. Once the correct balance has been achieved and it has become second-nature in our playing, then is the time to trust it, let it go, and think only of the music. But the analysis/experimentation is crucial and must come first.

Deliberate Practice

So now we have entered the area of "deliberate practice." In the March 2017 issue of Nautilus, author Alex Sojourn-Kim Pang references several studies that explored the nature of successful practice. One such study focused on violin students in a Berlin music conservatory in the 1980's. Authors Ericsson, Krampe, and Tesch-Römer noted in
their study that the difference between the great students and the average ones was that not only did the great students practice more, but they also practiced in a more <u>deliberate</u> way. In other words,

the great students were not mindlessly watching the clock as they repeated exercise after exercise. Ericsson stated that the great students were "engaging with full concentration." They were paying close attention to details, and had clear goals in mind. Pang went on to summarize their findings by saying that "deliberate practice isn't a lot of fun, and it's not immediately profitable. It means being in the pool before sunrise,…practicing fingering or breathing in a windowless room, spending hours perfecting details that only a few other people will ever notice." He went on to say that if you are intent on greatness at what you do, you will embrace the discipline necessary for deliberate practice "because it reinforces your sense of who you are and who you will become."

A quick scan of the paragraph above will reveal phrases such as "full concentration" and "attention to details" and "clear goals" and "discipline," all of which are critical if you are to achieve your goal of finding your correct trumpet playing balance. This deliberate way of practicing can be mentally taxing, so it is important for you to work toward a very disciplined approach in terms of scheduling of practice sessions, prioritizing practice above other activities, carefully planning you practice activities, taking care of your mental and physical health, getting enough rest, and so forth. This requires sacrifice, for there is no easy path on this journey. Unless you place a high priority on this important work, you will have to be willing to accept a much lesser level of achievement. Do not delude yourself that you can reach your full potential the easy way. It just won't happen.

Finding Your Balance

Now allow me to make a few suggestions as you undertake deliberate practice in your quest for your correct playing balance.

When- The best time to practice is in the morning. This is when you are at your best. If you believe that you are not a morning person, think again. If you are taking care of yourself, eating well, getting to bed at a decent hour, then you will find the morning hours to be your best. Schedule your practice session in blocks of no more that 45-60 minutes. Then take a break. It has been shown that 2-3 sessions divided by periods of rest are better than one long practice session. Also, do not attempt to play constantly without stopping during these sessions. It is better to take your time. This will give you a chance to rest and reflect on each exercise.

Where- Find a place dedicated only to your practice. It is better to not pick your practice space just for convenience. Instead, find a space where you will not be interrupted by people or extraneous sounds, where you feel safe and comfortable. This should be perceived as a sort of "sacred" place you enter with an attitude of reverence and seriousness to engage in important work. The Greeks had a word for this type of place: TEMENOS. A "temenos" is a place dedicated to one specific activity such as worship or meditation. You practice should be as focused as when you meditate or worship, for only with this kind of attitude will you be successful in fully reaching your goals.

How- As you enter your practice space, begin to quiet your mind, blocking out all thoughts except those regarding the task at hand. A few moments of relaxed deep breaths will help you clear your head.

In your first few attempts of this deliberate practice, work on honing your observation skills without your instrument. Simply let your "mind's eye" move to various parts of your body, observing each part briefly. Ask yourself, "What does my left ear feel like right now? My right pinkie finger? My right elbow? What are my ribs doing as I breathe deeply?" By doing this exercise, you will soon find that you can quickly move your attention and focus to most portions of your body. Now it is time to apply this skill as you practice your instrument. Begin by playing simple scalar or lip slur exercises while making very general observations:

1. How does it feel? (The less effort, the better.)
2. How does it sound? (Always strive for the best sound.)

Why are these thoughts important? Asking yourself how your playing feels or sounds will immediately force you into the mode of observation. Only if you observe the feeling and the sound can you begin to more specifically analyze what you are experiencing.

Next, begin observing the vibration point (lips). Are the lips vibrating freely? If not, you will hear that in your sound. Several things could be at play here. Perhaps the vibration of the lips is inhibited by too much mouthpiece pressure, so ease off on that to see what happens. Perhaps it is due to too much tension at the point of the aperture. If so, let the aperture relax into a more open position. Perhaps the lips are not vibrating well due to a lack of airflow, in which case you simply increase the flow rate. If you determine that the air is not moving with enough energy, you will need to determine the root of the problem. Is it simply lack of blowing effort, or is there constriction at resistance points that need your attention? Once the air stream is working properly, shift your attention elsewhere such as to the tongue arch. Is it working optimally?

These are the types of observations and analyses that must be going through your mind as you practice, so start with the easiest of exercises such as long tones or slow lip slurs, or perhaps a simple scale or melodic phrase. Continue "tweaking" the various aspects of your playing until you find what you think is your proper balance. In other words, work toward the point at which your playing feels right and sounds right. Once you have found this balance, move on to more extended kinds of exercises, etudes, etc. Then, the next day, repeat the process. Remember, at this stage of your training, "analysis is definitely <u>NOT</u> paralysis." It is critical for developing the tools to be your own best teacher.

While it is true that this requires a good amount of concentration, you will discover that when you find that right balance for you, it will be very satisfying. You will know it when it happens because it will feel right and sound right. Your playing will seem more effortless. This may not happen every day at first, and once you find the balance, it may go away after a time. But that is OK. Keep trying each day to find that balance. Over time, it will become a challenge that you look forward to each day when you pick up your horn, and when you find it yet again, it will give you the assurance that you are on the right track to becoming a better player.

1. The Routine

I consider practice routines to be fluid, changing according to the needs of the student. However, I have found this routine effective as a starting point. Allow it to change as the student progresses.

A Flutter the lips for several seconds to encourage blood flow.

B mouthpiece alone — Produce a sound that is well-centered and focused.

Cont. downward chromatically.

C Play on the trumpet.

D on Trumpet, ♩ = 100 — Try to achieve a sound that is lively and strong. Settle for nothing less than your best sound. DO NOT rush through this! Take your time.

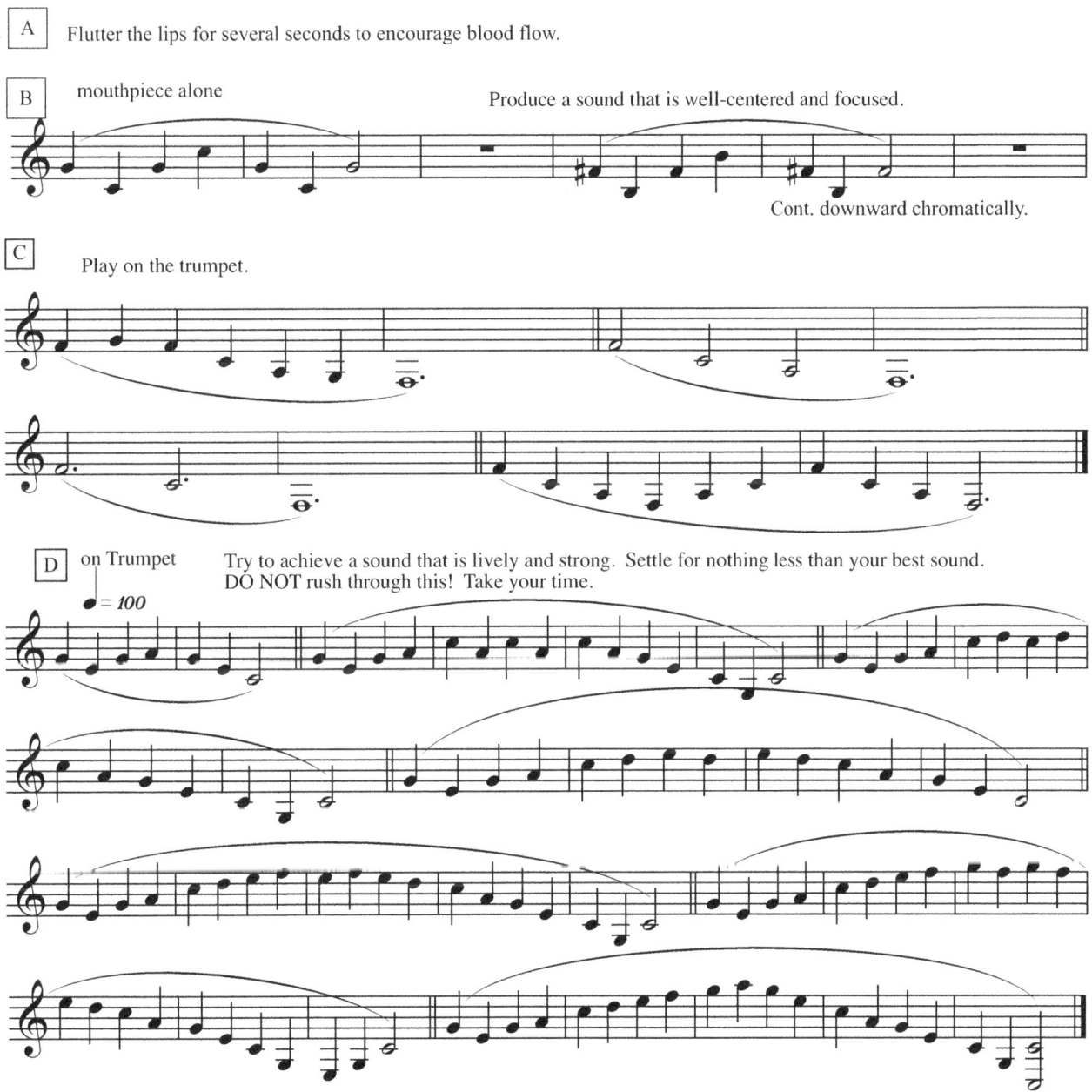

E — Be sure to use the same fingering throughout each phrase.

Think "down" as you ascend, think "up" as you descend.

F — Be sure to use the same fingering throughout each phrase.

G — Be sure to use the same fingering throughout each phrase.

H — Be sure to use the same fingering throughout each phrase.

Think "down" as you ascend, think "up" as you descend.

Continue upward chromatically.
This is where the "money" is!

2. Remedial Routine

Utilize this routine if you are coming back from a layoff or if you are trying to work out embouchure problems. The concept here is to keep things very simple to encourage success, which will in turn build confidence. This routine can also be used as a routine for a beginning student.

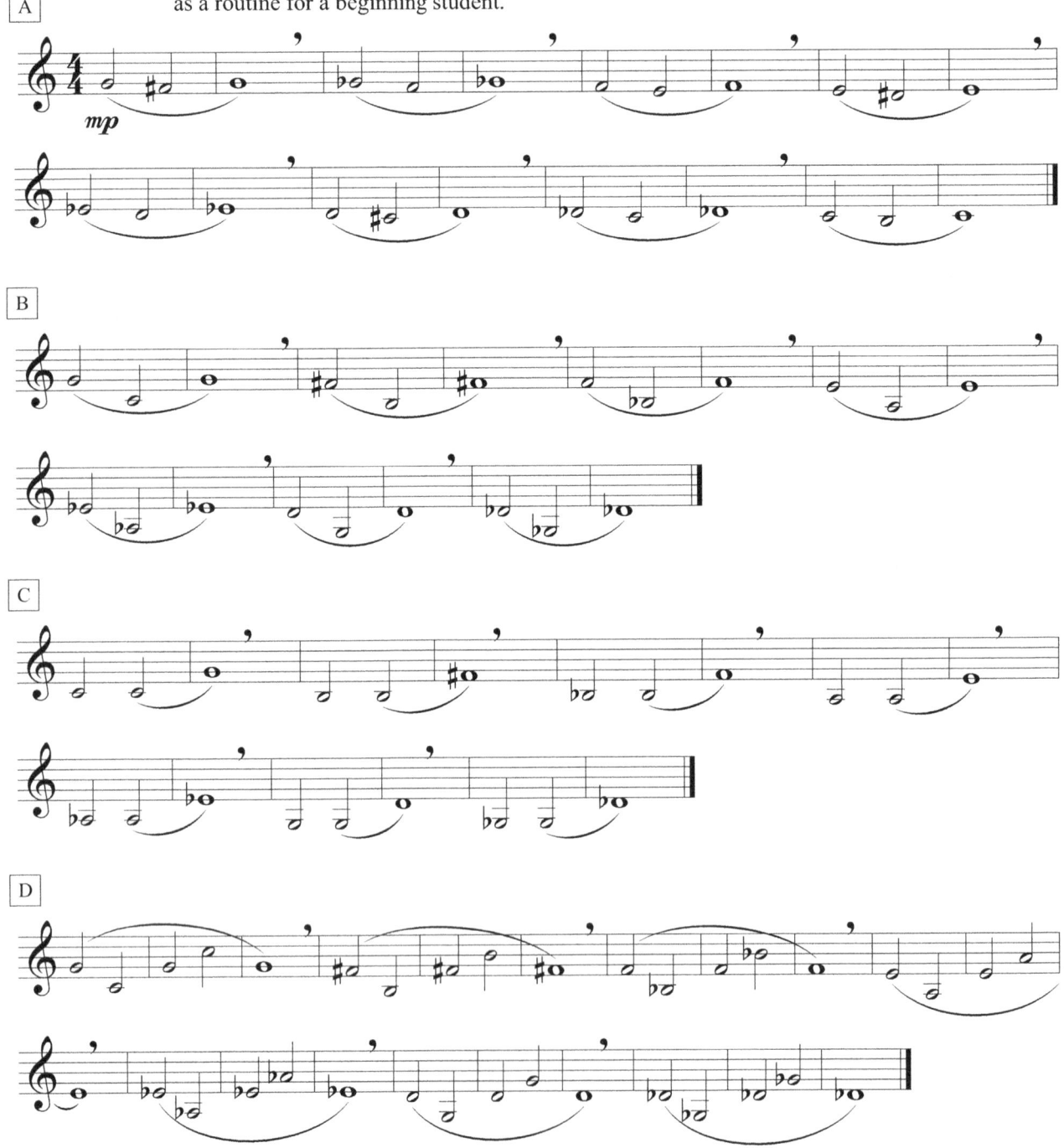

3. Melodic Phrases

4. The Joy of Breathing

Play with a full sound, take full breaths, and use up all of the air.

1st time: do the shorter phrases (Eighth note= 100).....2nd time: do the longer phrases (Eighth note= 132)
3rd time: try playing it all in one breath! (Dotted quarter note= 80)
REST BETWEEN EACH ONE.

A Don't think "toooooo...", think "t-HOOOOOOOO"!

B. Tongue the following version, but imagine that you are slurring as in the previous one. (Eighth note=160)

5. Embouchure Studies
Group I

6. Embouchure Studies
Group II

7. Embouchure Studies
Group III

E-2

Continue chromatically upward with same exercise.

F

Accelerate the air through the horn. Think "forward" with the sound.

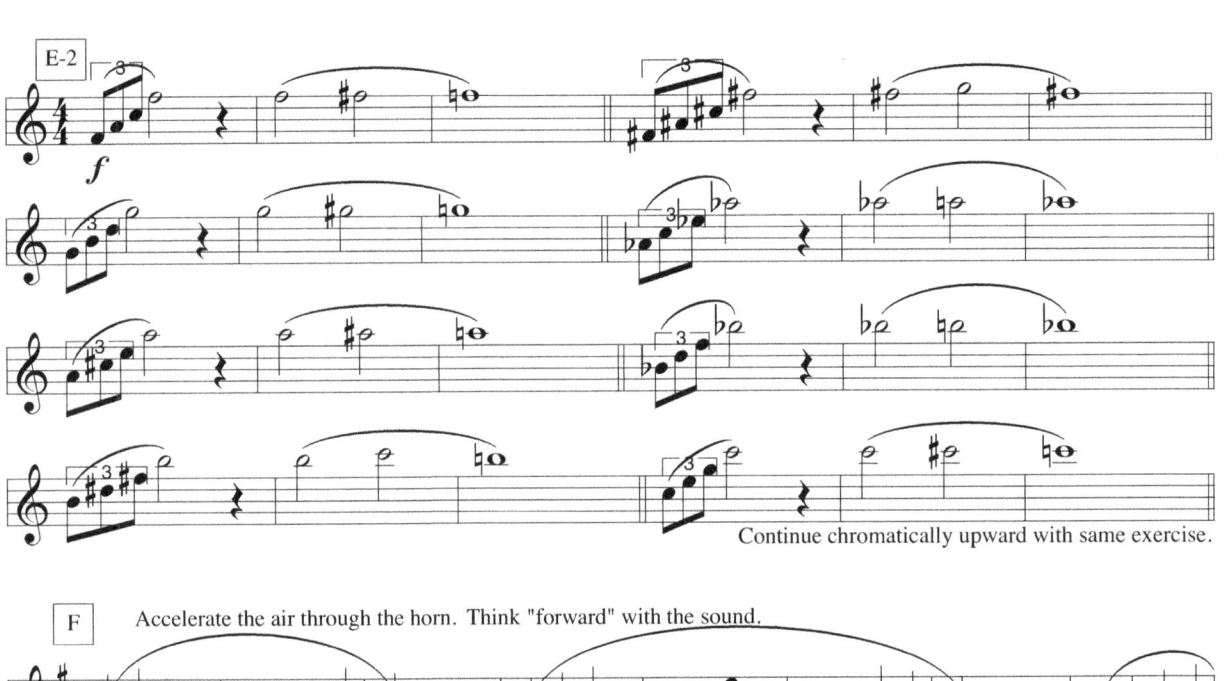

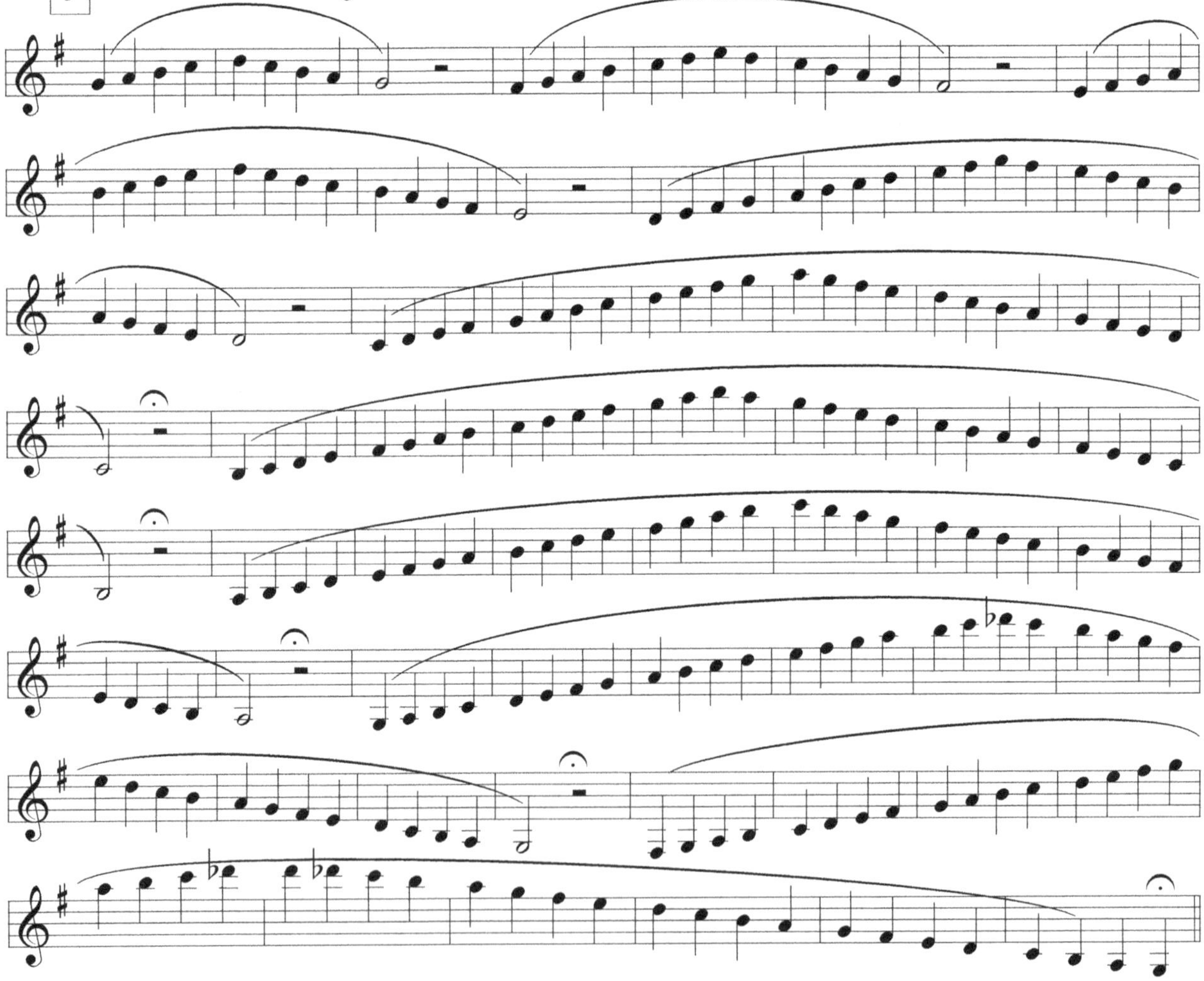

Continue chromatically upward with same exercise.

8. Pedal Tone Study

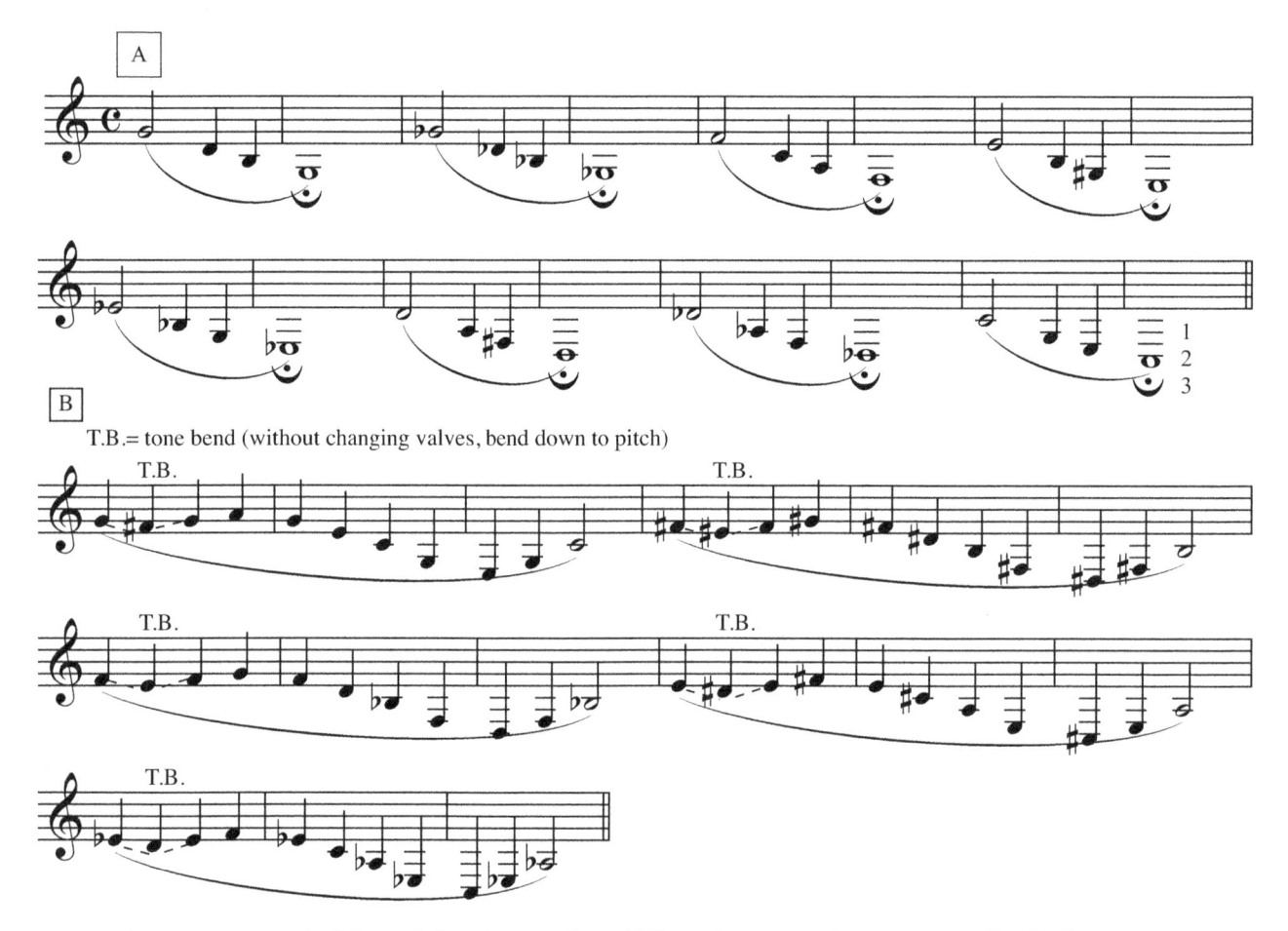

T.B. = tone bend (without changing valves, bend down to pitch)

As you move out of the pedal register to the middle and upper register, try to maintain the same puckered setting. Think "lip thickness" not "lip tension" as you ascend. Also, think "down" when you ascend, and "up" when you descend. This may be difficult at first, but will soon be mastered.

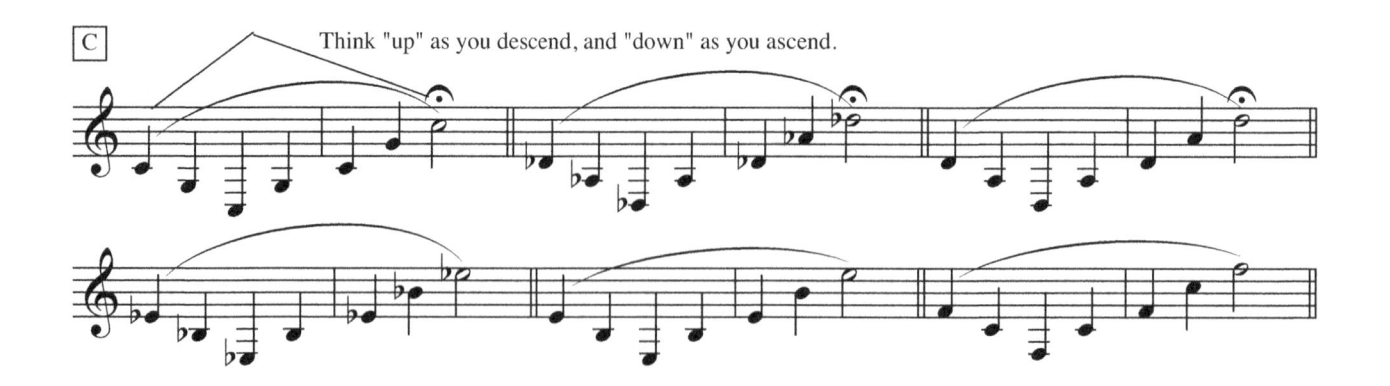

Think "up" as you descend, and "down" as you ascend.

| D |

Cont. upward chromatically...

| E | Sub-pedals

The embouchure should not change significantly here.

9. Single Tonguing

[F]

[G]

[H]

Alternate articulation: Do all the preceding exercises with the following articulation pattern...

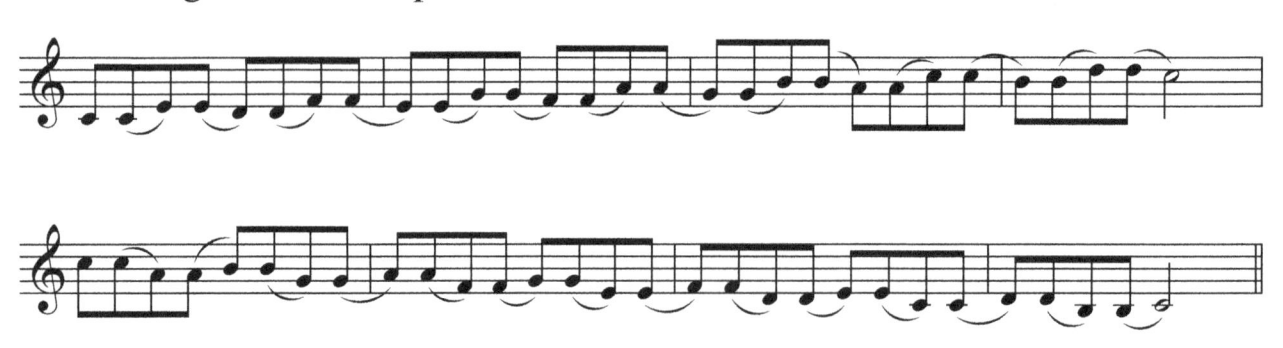

Practice both marcato and legato tonguing on long, short, loud, and soft notes.

Practice the following exercises utilizing various combinations of the three variables explored above (ie. volume, note length, articulation strength)

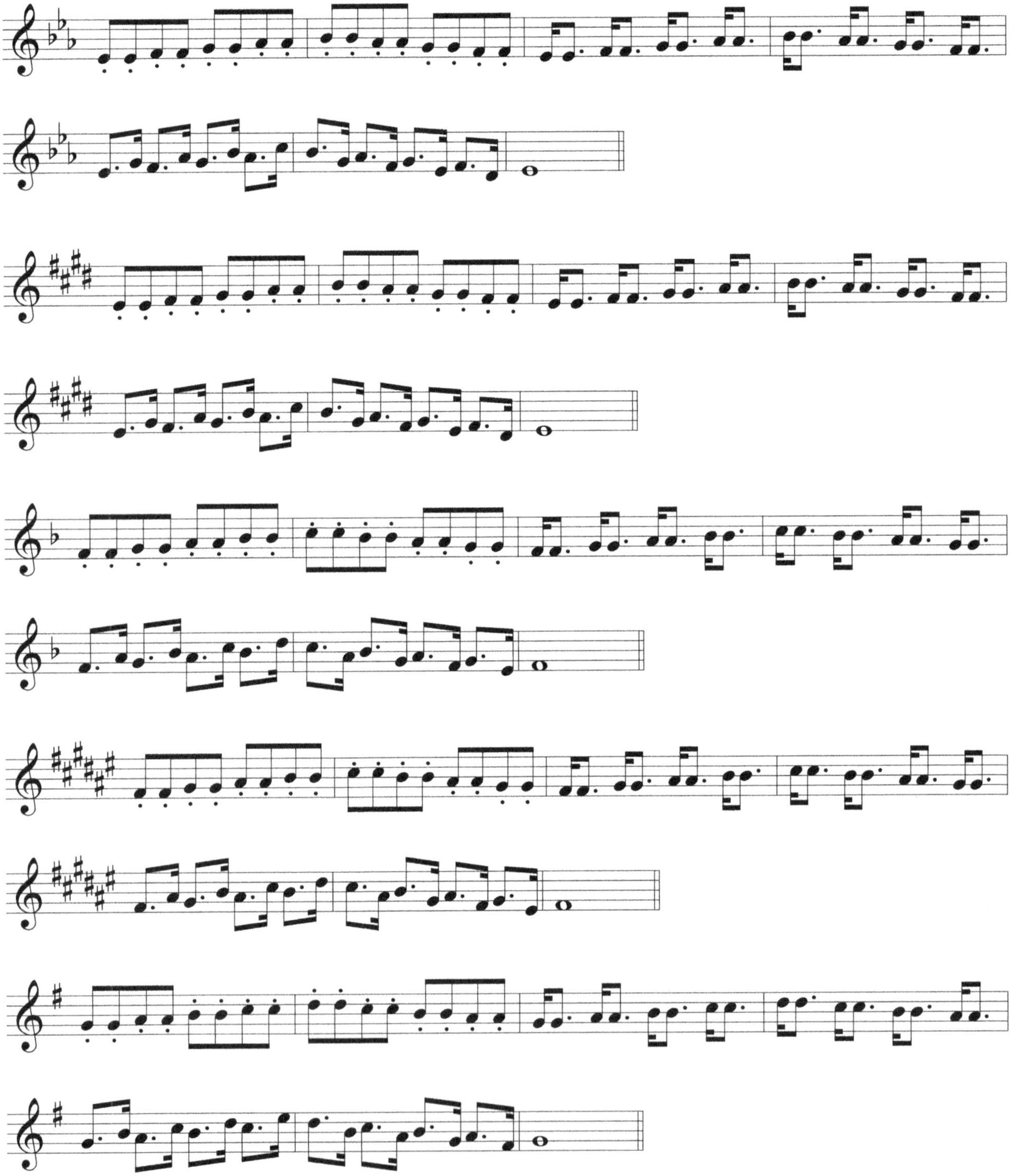

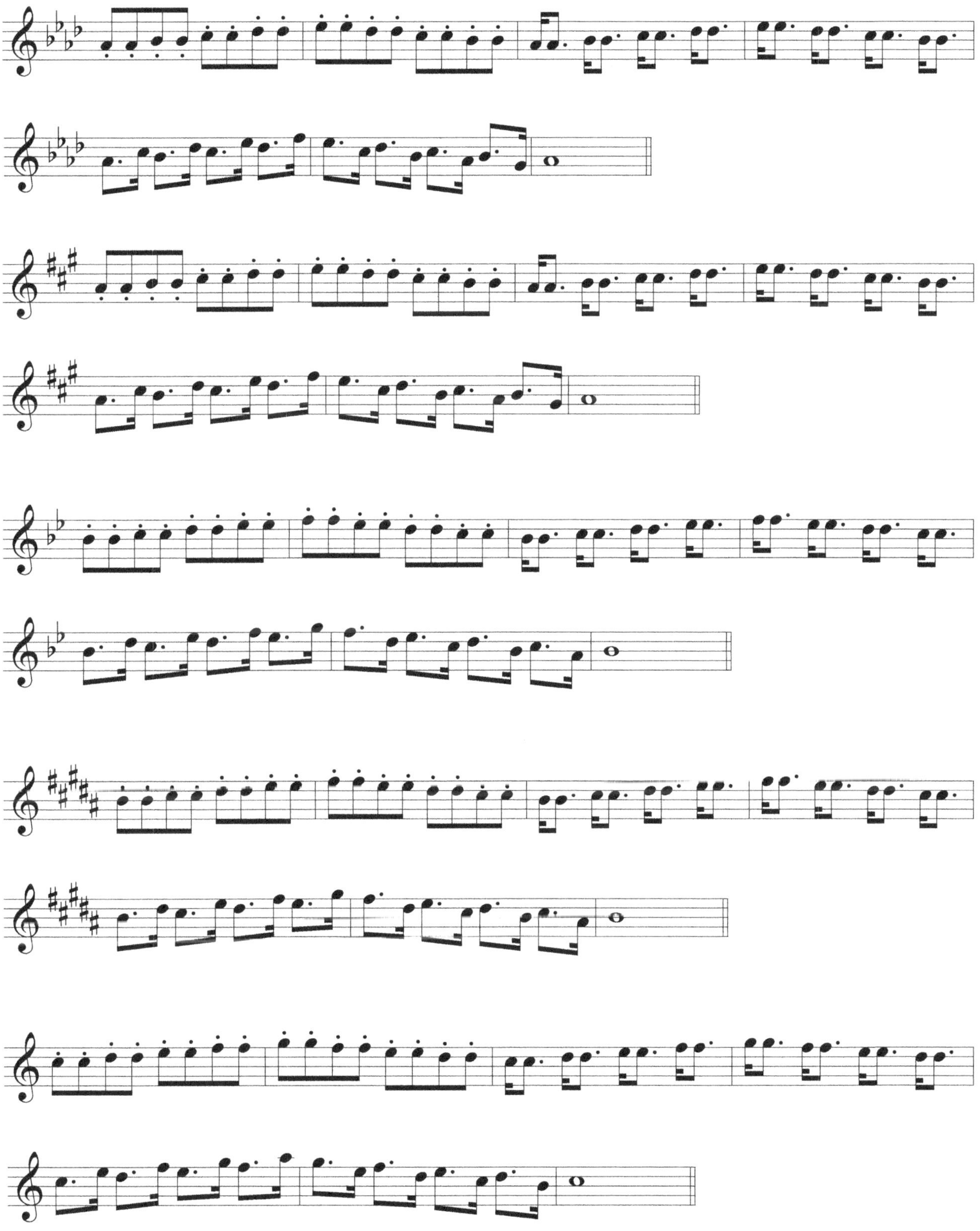

10. Multiple Tonguing

A Triple Tongue

47

G

Double Tongue

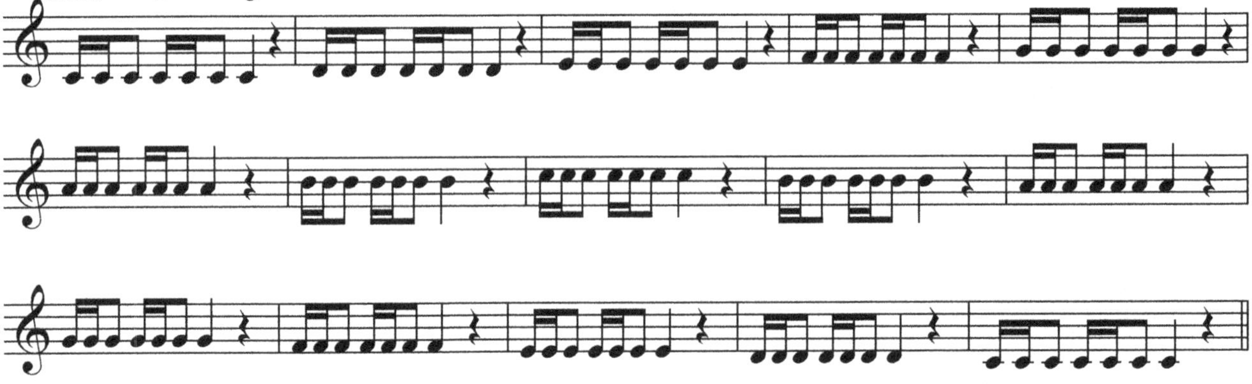

H

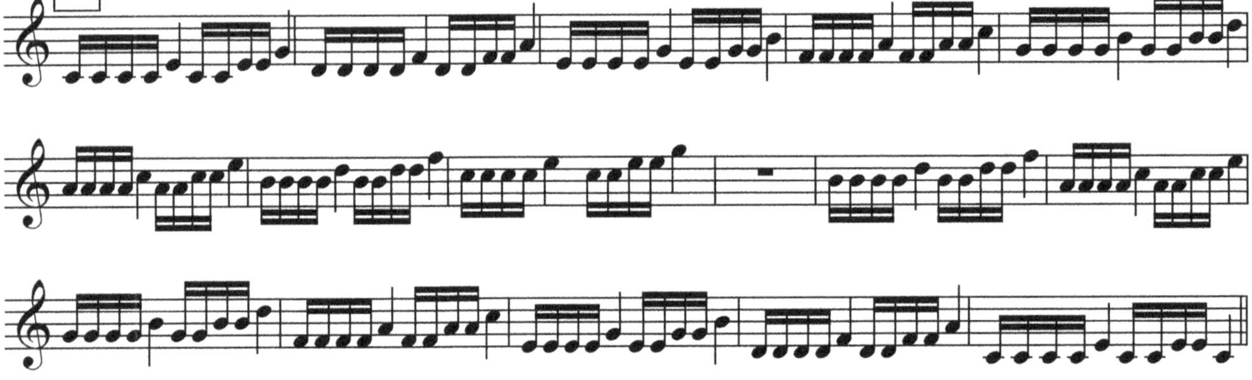

I

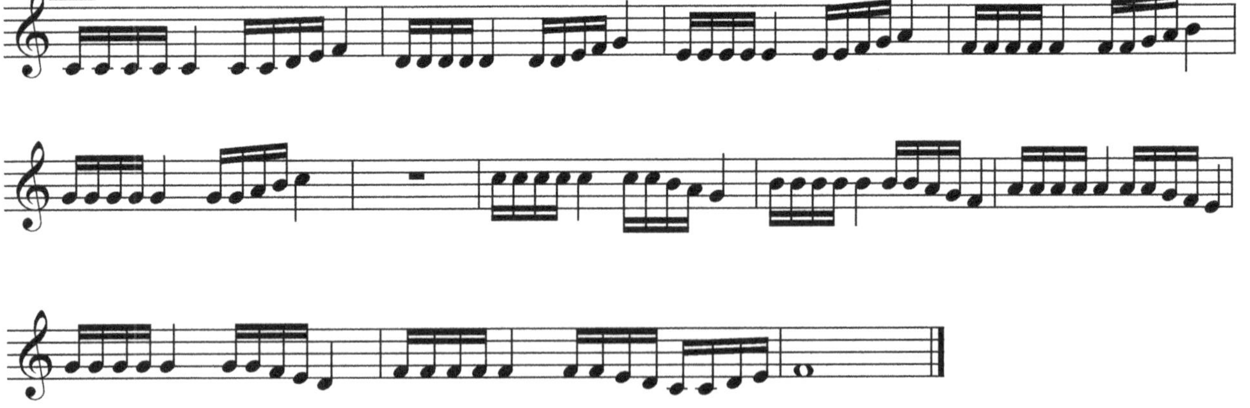

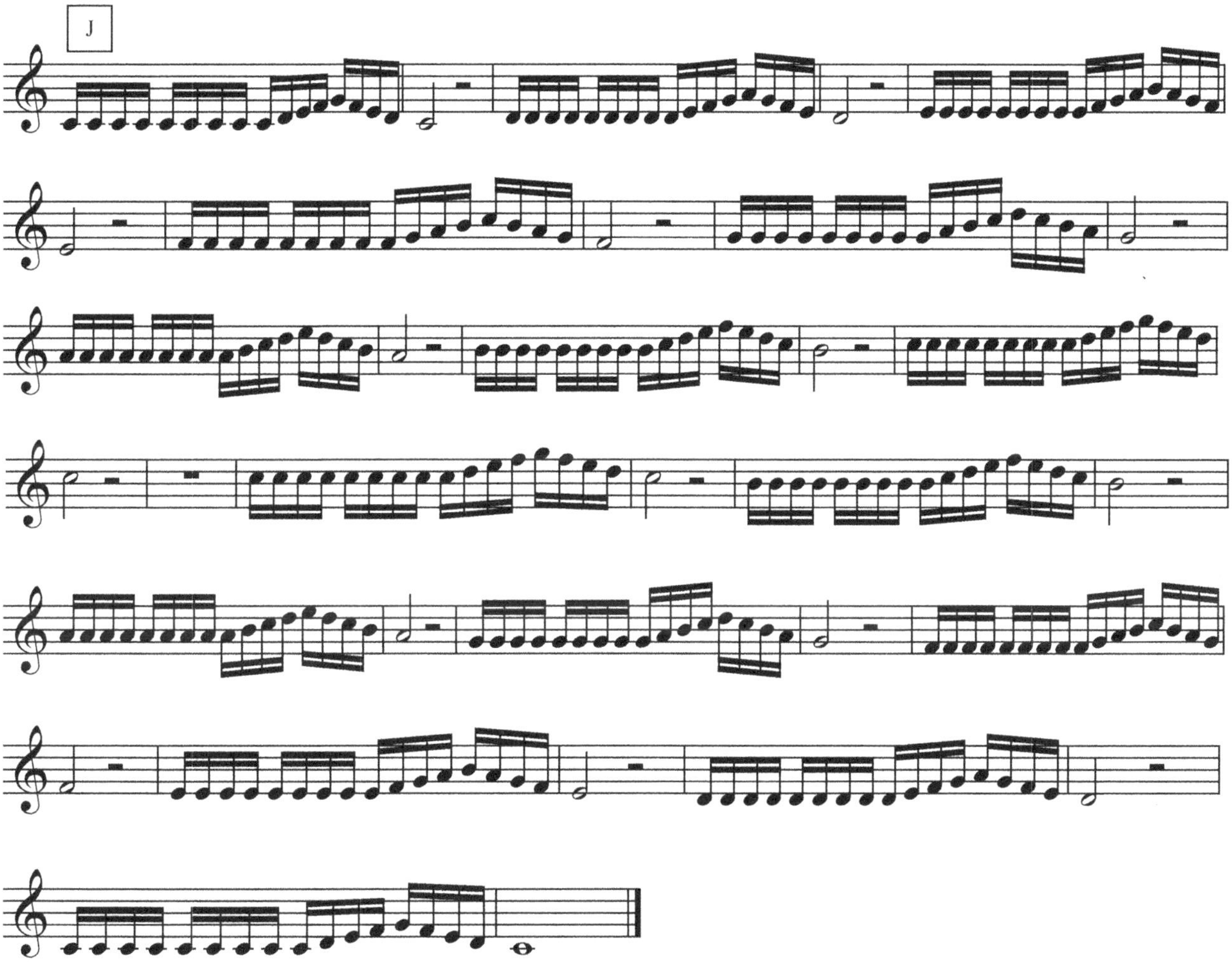
J

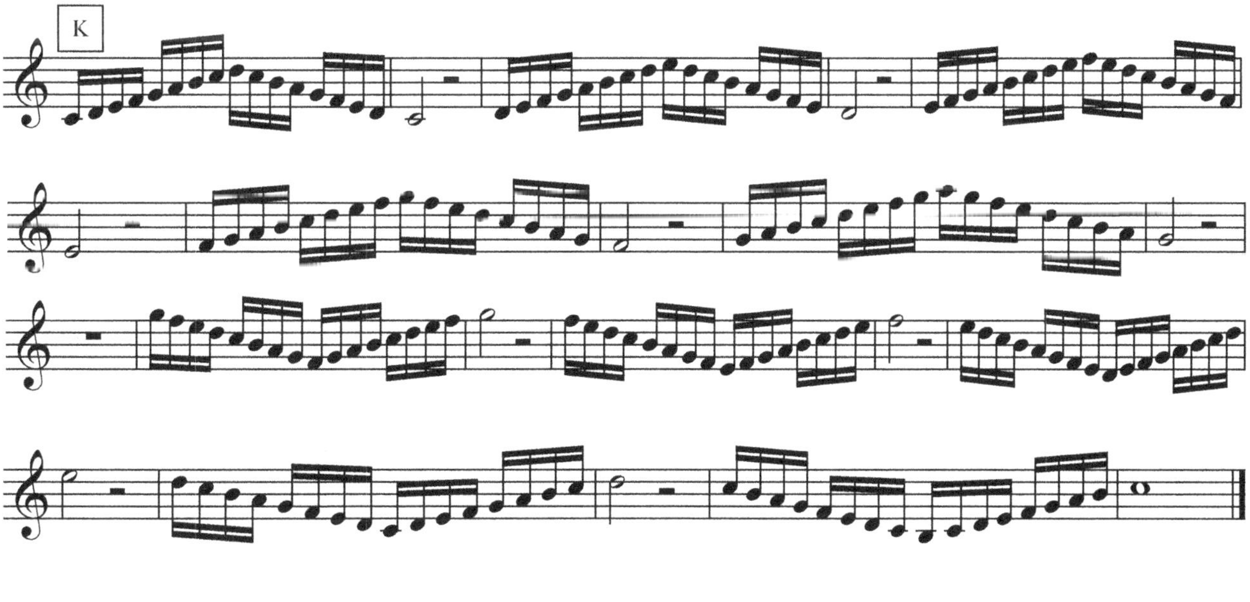
K

11. Accuracy Studies

A — Slowly, use metronome, reset mthpce. for each measure

D — Random pitches

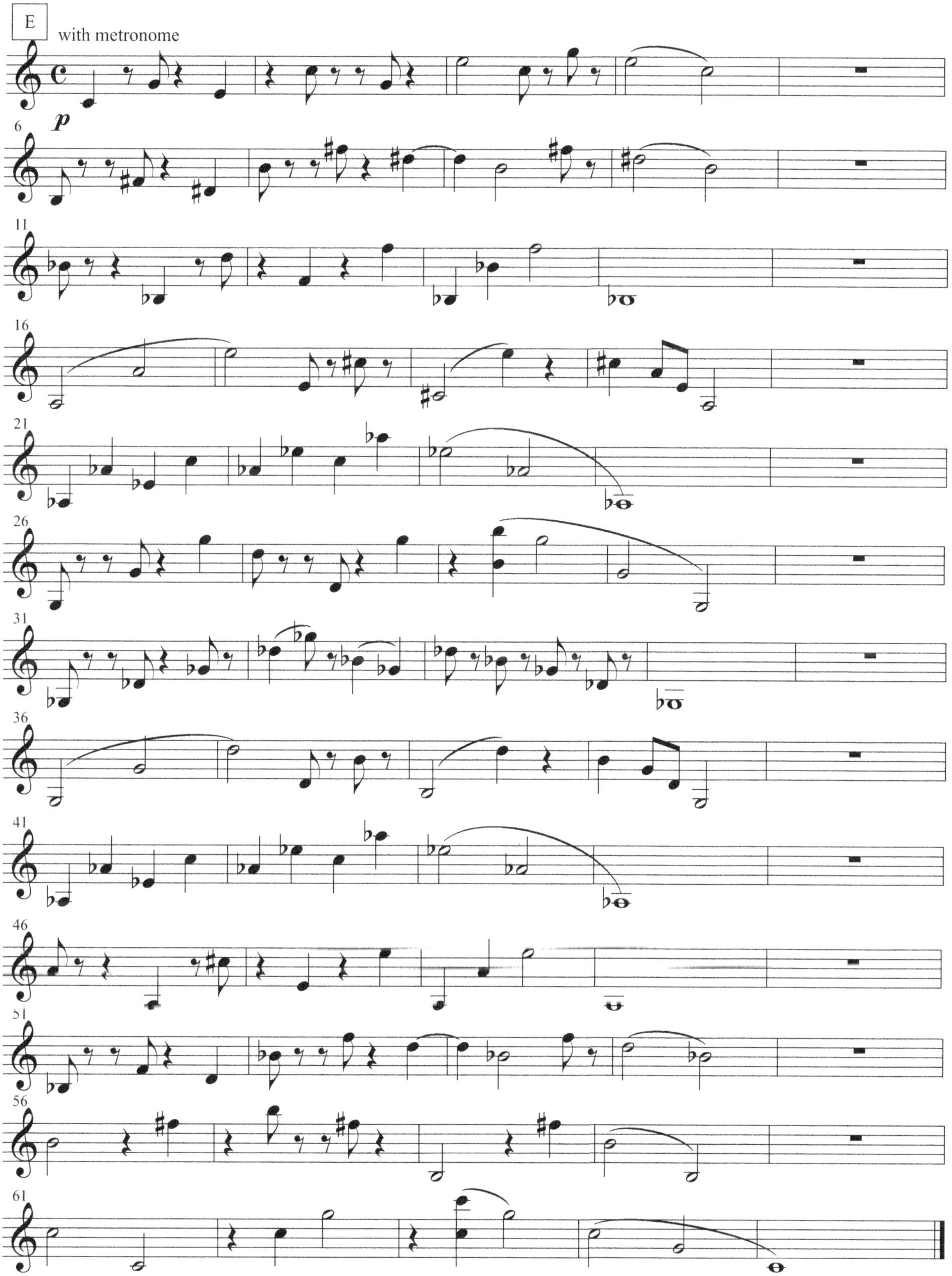
E
with metronome
p

12. Long-setting Exercises
(use metronome)

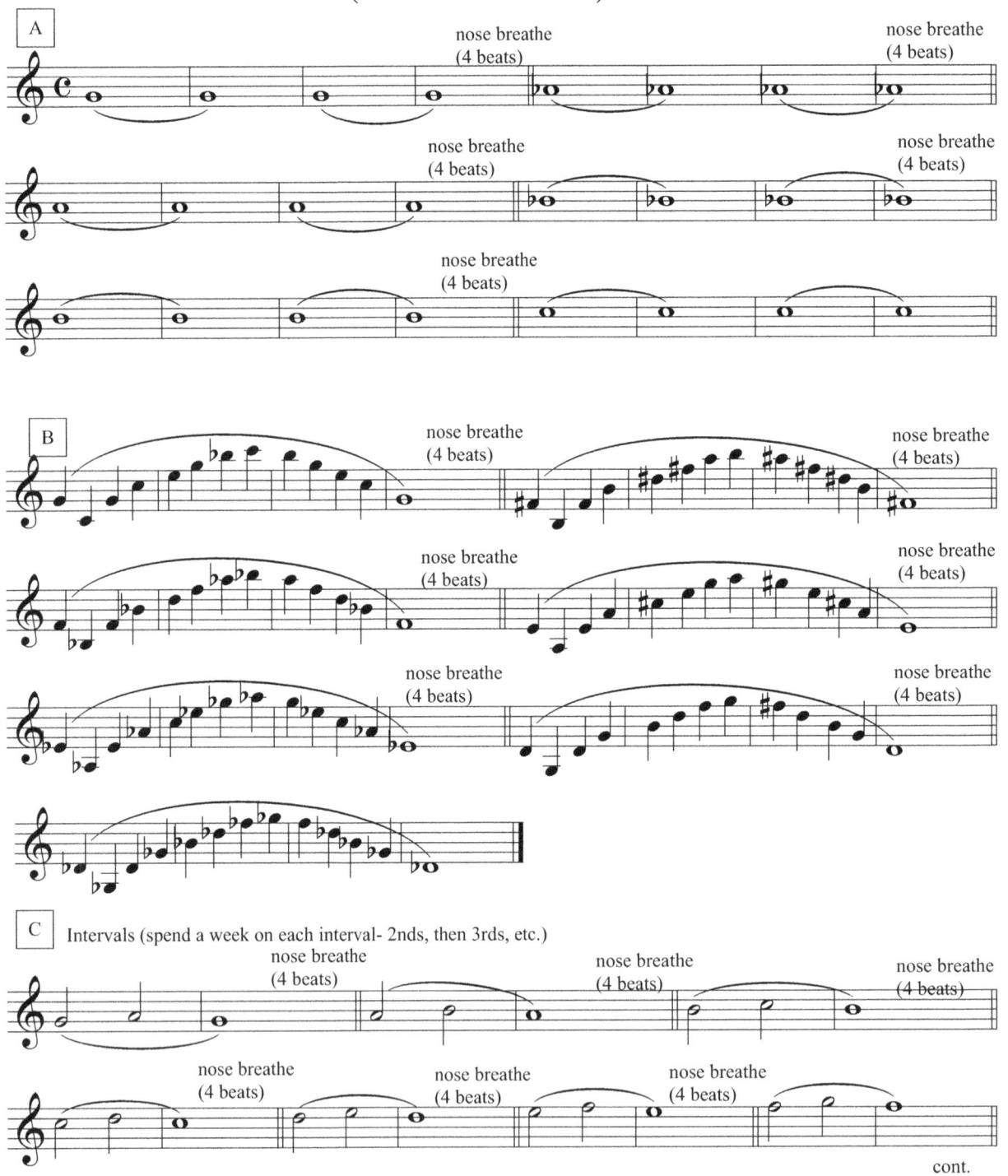

13. Tone Bending

Tone bending helps to gain better control of the aperture, resulting in a more relaxed, resonant sound. These exercises can also be used as preliminary exercises for pedal tone work.

54

14. Tuning Etudes

Tune up using your tuner.
As you play these etudes, hold each fermata. When you think you are in tune, check your intonation on the tuner to see how close you are. Then proceed.

15. Fingers

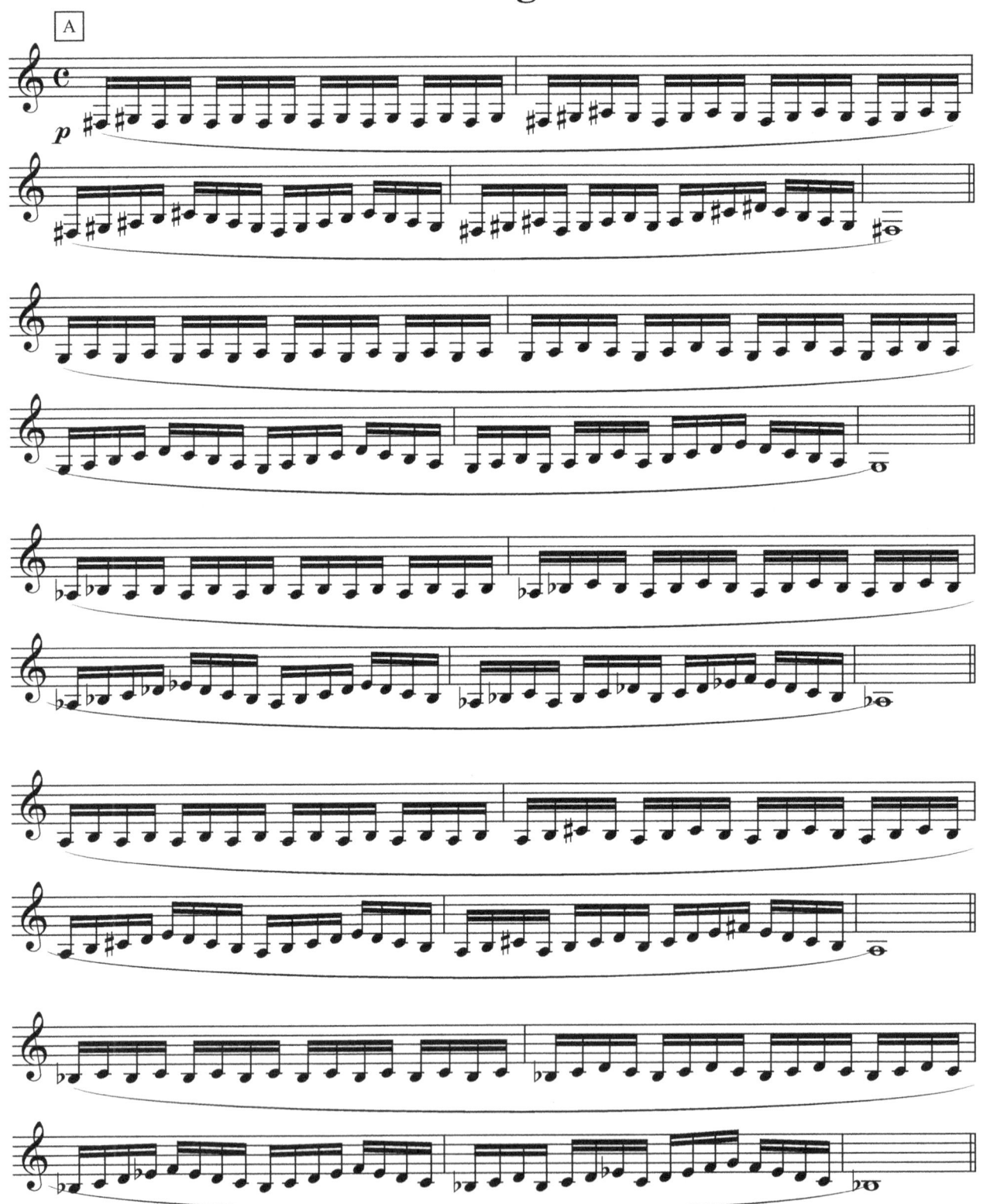

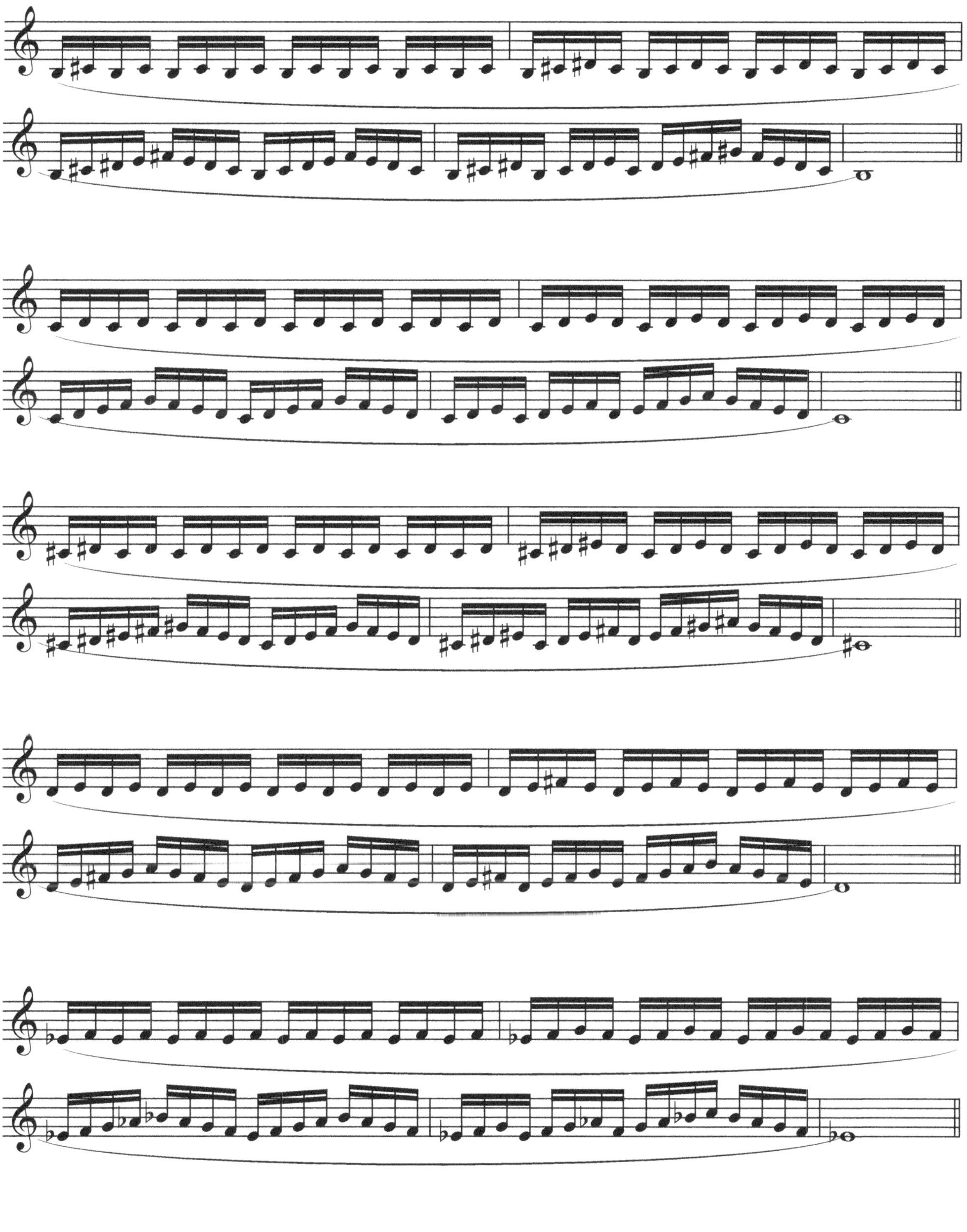

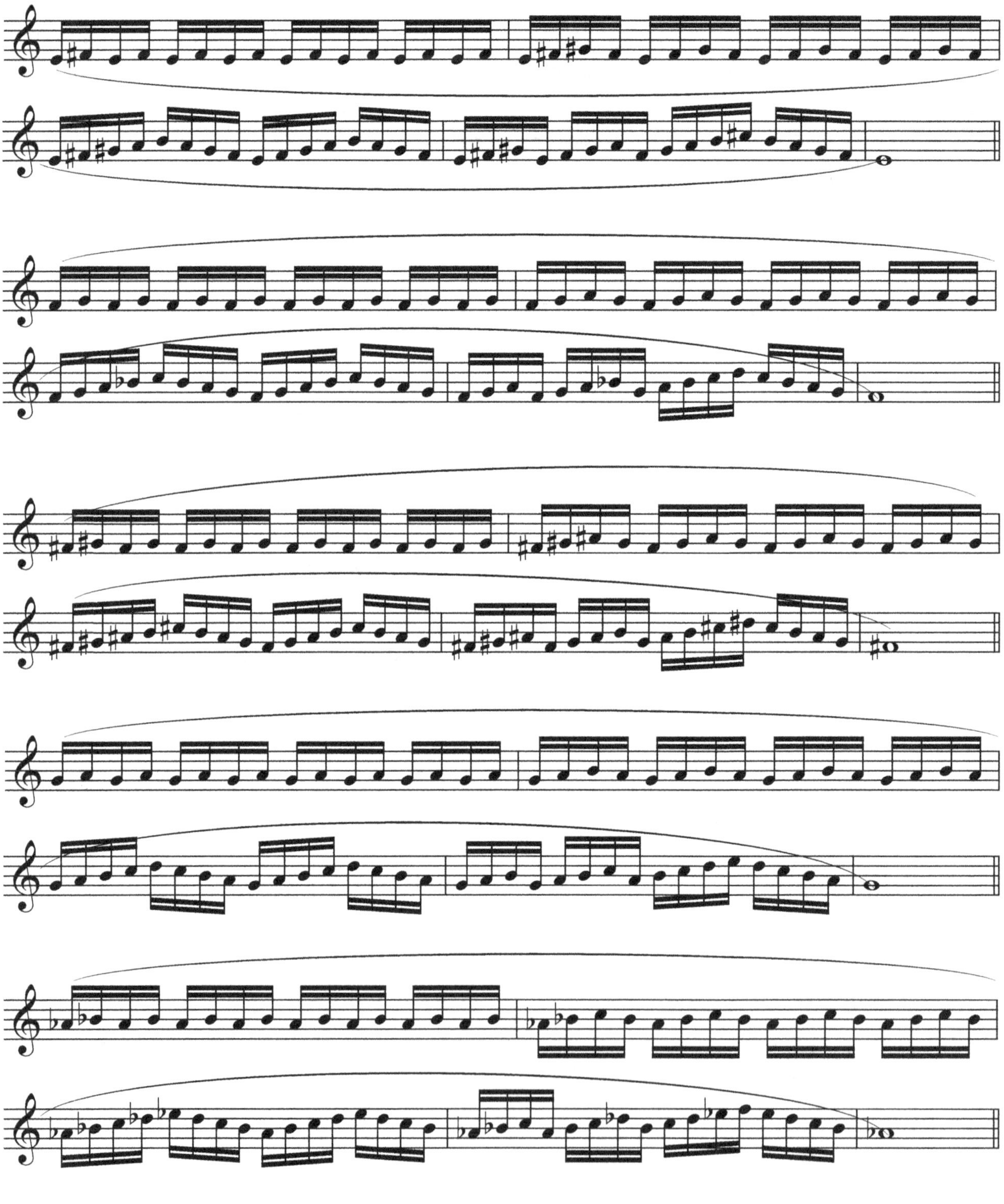

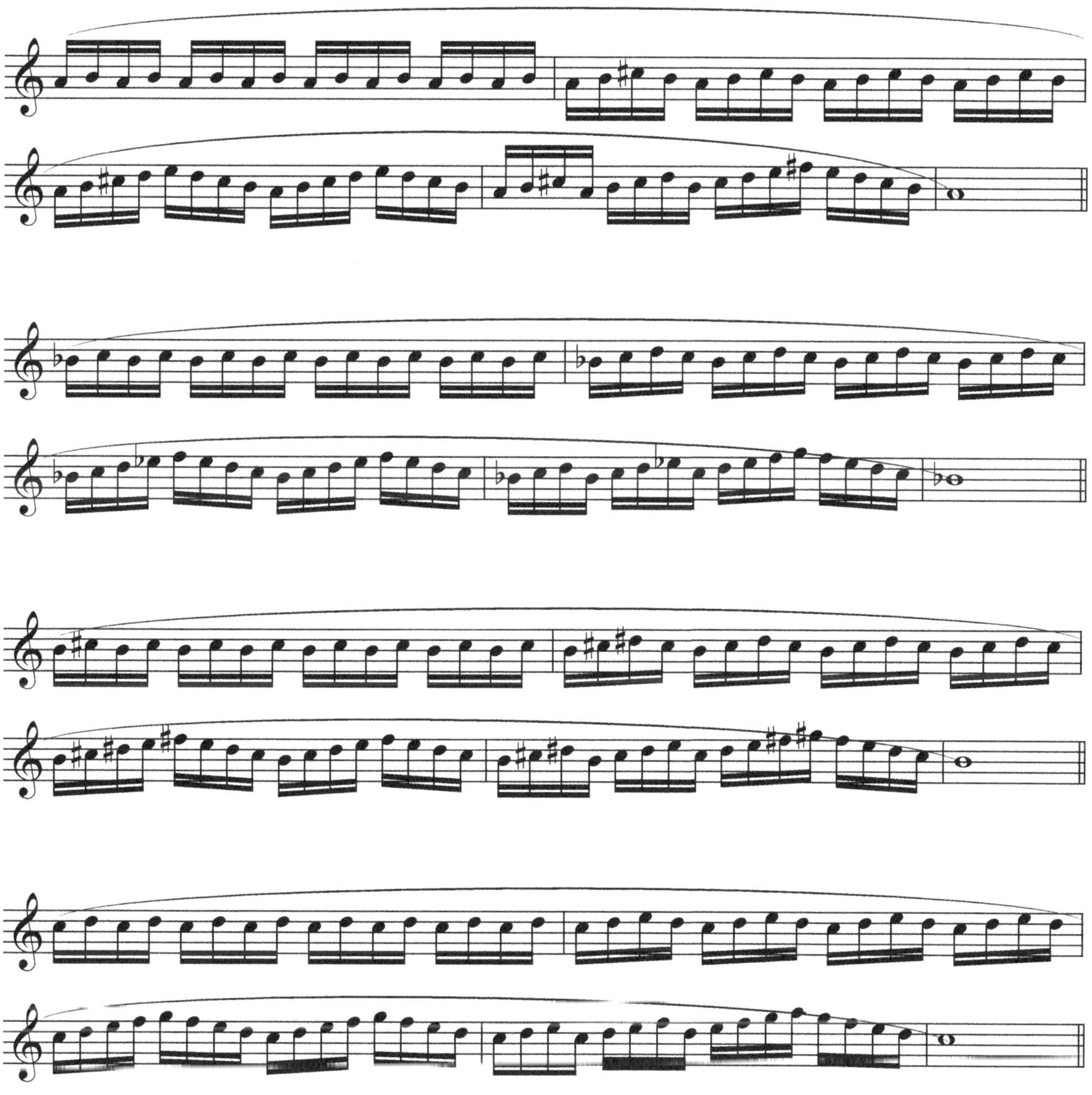

Continue upward....

16. Chromatics

A Slowly at first.....play with a big, full sound always!! Accelerate the air through the horn.

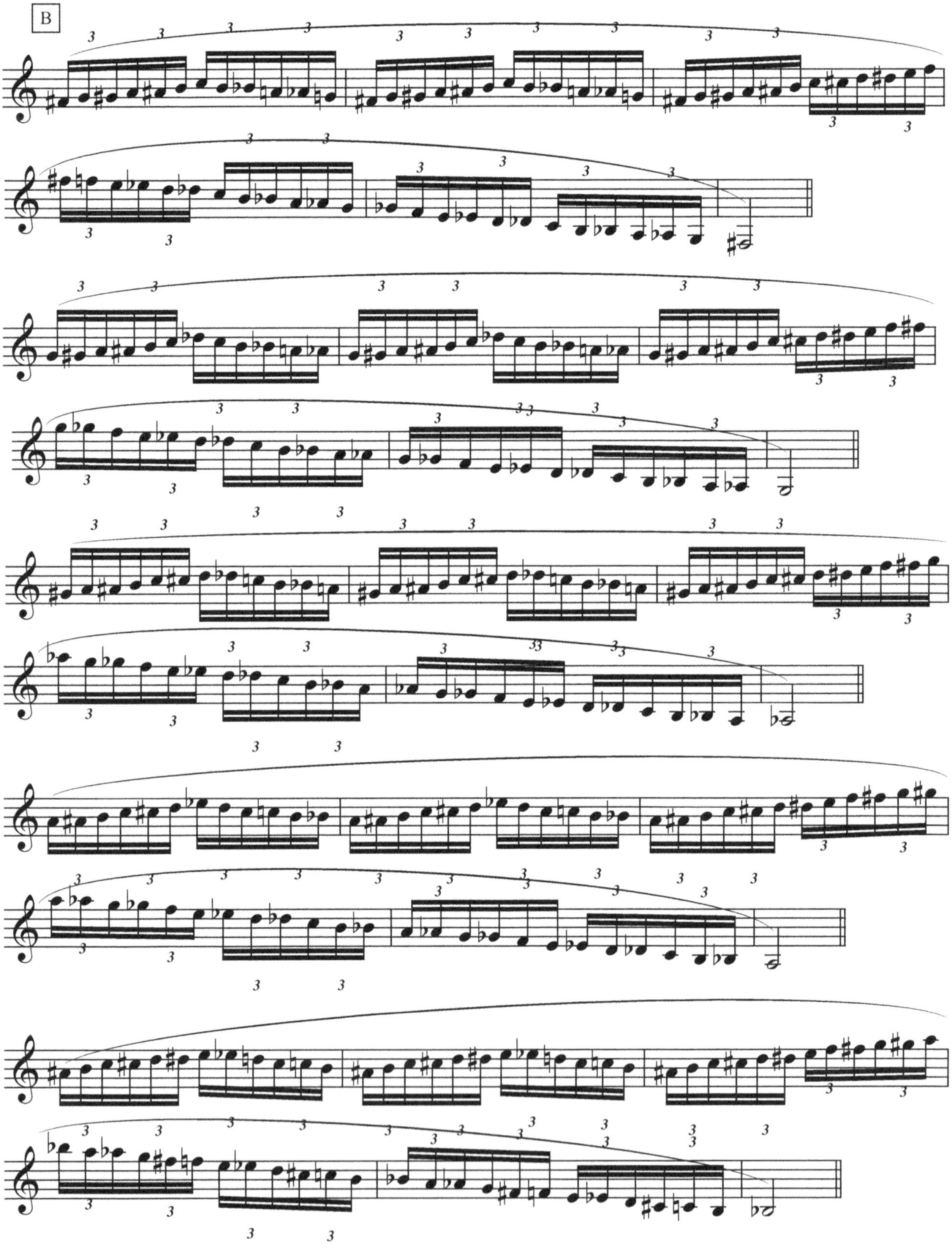
B

63

17. Vibrato Study

To achieve a good hand vibrato, move the right hand slightly back and forth, but not so much that the movement is preceptible to the eye.

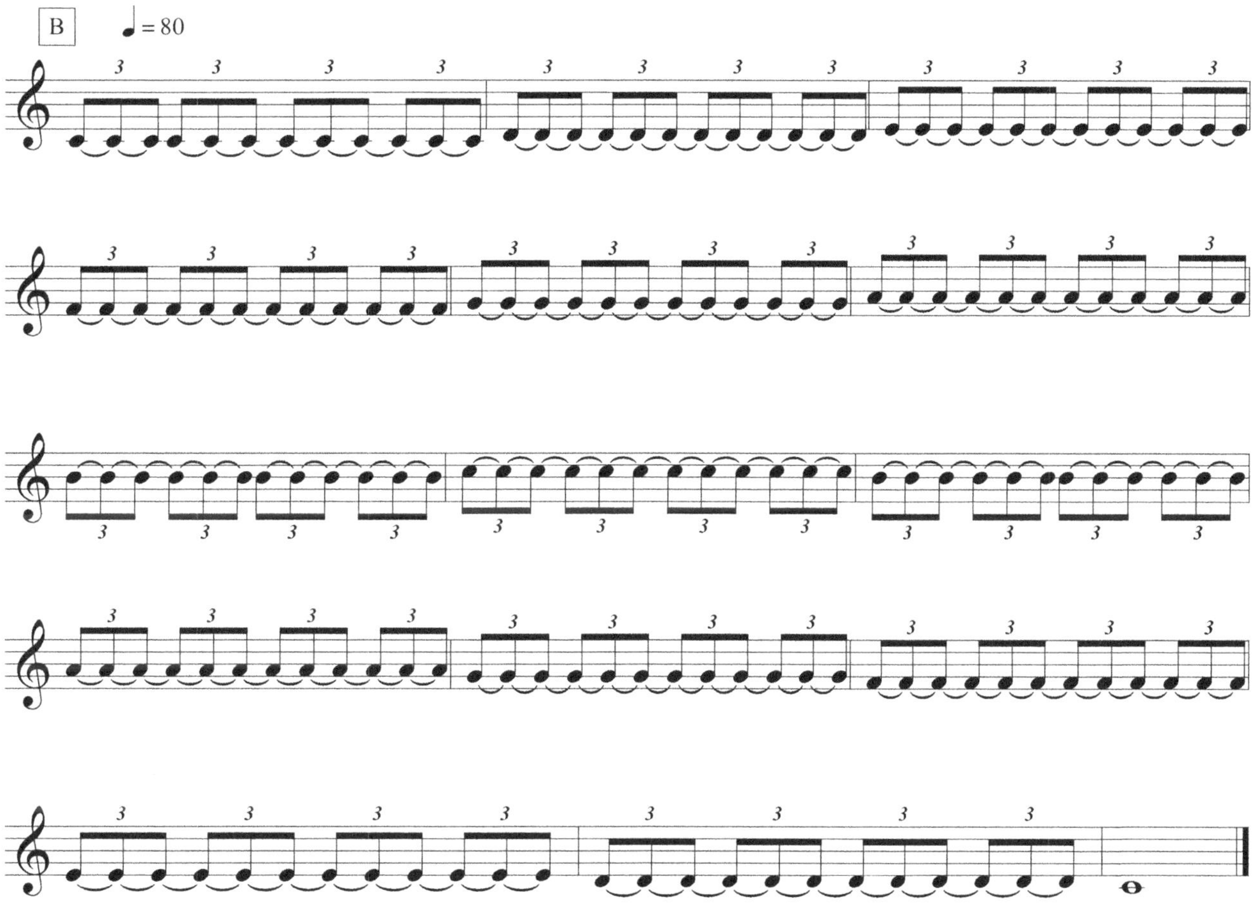
B
♩= 80

18. Jazz Patterns

Use progressions A and B for practicing patterns 1-13 below.

A

| Dmin7 | G7 | CMaj7 | CMaj7 | Cmin7 | F7 | B♭Maj7 | B♭Maj7 |

| B♭min7 | E♭7 | A♭Maj7 | A♭Maj7 | A♭min7 | D♭7 | G♭Maj7 | G♭Maj7 |

| F♯min7 | B7 | EMaj7 | EMaj7 | Emin7 | A7 | DMaj7 | DMaj7 |

B

| C♯min7 | F♯7 | BMaj7 | BMaj7 | Bmin7 | E7 | AMaj7 | AMaj7 |

| Amin7 | D7 | GMaj7 | GMaj7 | Gmin7 | C7 | FMaj7 | FMaj7 |

| Fmin7 | B♭7 | E♭Maj7 | E♭Maj7 | E♭min7 | A♭7 | D♭Maj7 | D♭Maj7 |

1. Dmin7 | G7 | CMaj7

2.

3.

4.

5.

6. starting on the 3rd

7. chromatic neighbors

8.

9. chromatic passing tone

10. chromatic passing tones

11.

12. Altered 9ths

13. Enclosure around 5th

19. Playing Over Changes

Improvise 8th note lines over the following progression. Start with chord tones and later add passing tones.

EXAMPLES....The following are two examples of the kinds of lines you should be playing. Use primarily 8th notes as you repeat the progression over and over.

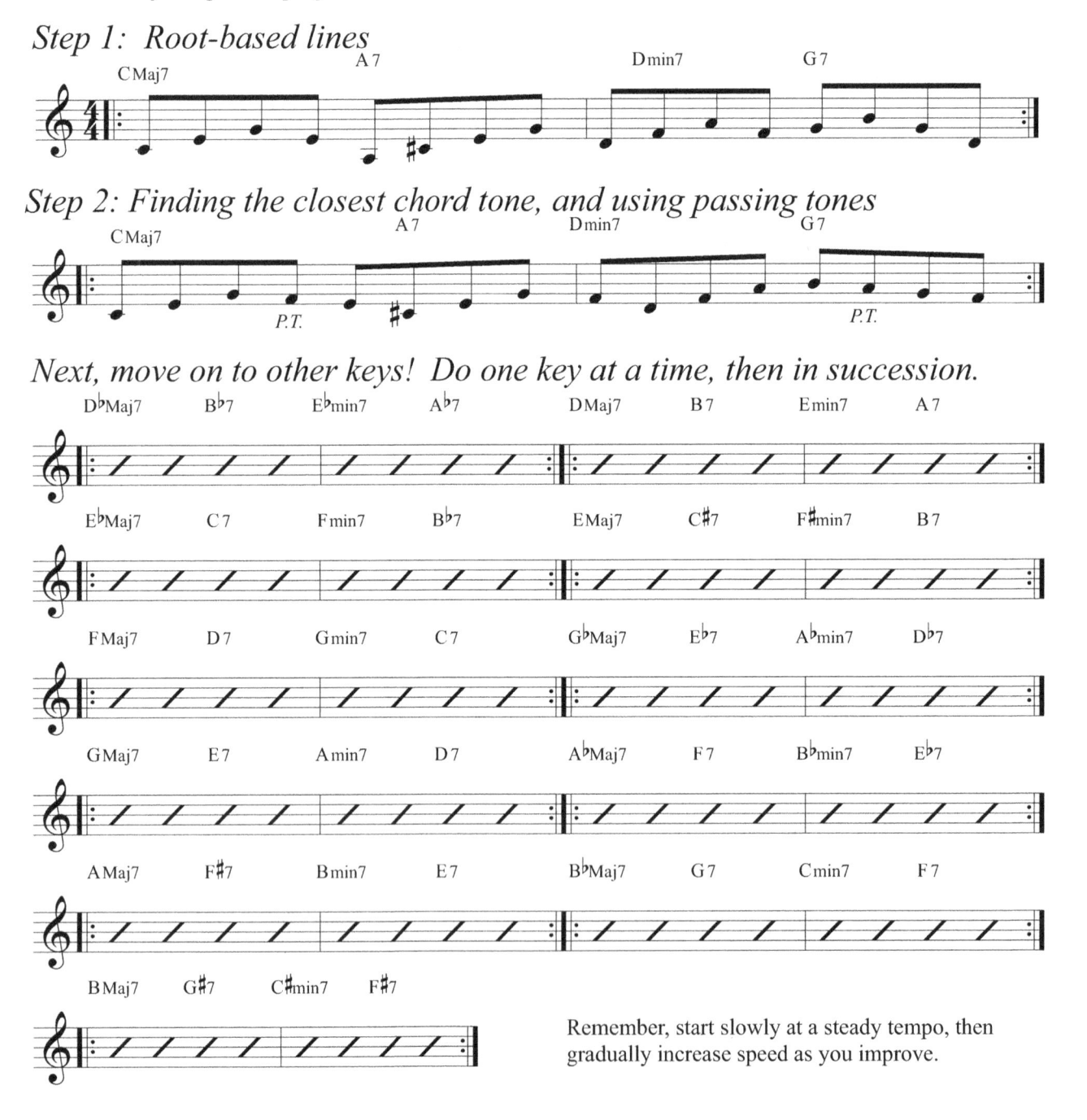

Step 1: Root-based lines

[Musical notation: CMaj7 | A7 | Dmin7 | G7]

Step 2: Finding the closest chord tone, and using passing tones

[Musical notation: CMaj7 | A7 | Dmin7 | G7, with P.T. markings]

Next, move on to other keys! Do one key at a time, then in succession.

D♭Maj7	B♭7	E♭min7	A♭7	DMaj7	B7	Emin7	A7
E♭Maj7	C7	Fmin7	B♭7	EMaj7	C#7	F#min7	B7
FMaj7	D7	Gmin7	C7	G♭Maj7	E♭7	A♭min7	D♭7
GMaj7	E7	Amin7	D7	A♭Maj7	F7	B♭min7	E♭7
AMaj7	F#7	Bmin7	E7	B♭Maj7	G7	Cmin7	F7
BMaj7	G#7	C#min7	F#7

Remember, start slowly at a steady tempo, then gradually increase speed as you improve.

Patterns to Practice for #19

Root-based

Any chord tone

Chromatic approach tones from below

Chromatic approach tones from above

Root position triads

Starting on the 3rd

7th chords (ascending)

7th chords (descending)

Passing tones

More passing tones

Next, improvise lines as in the following example, using concepts from above....

etc...

20. Jazz Progressions

Rhythm Changes

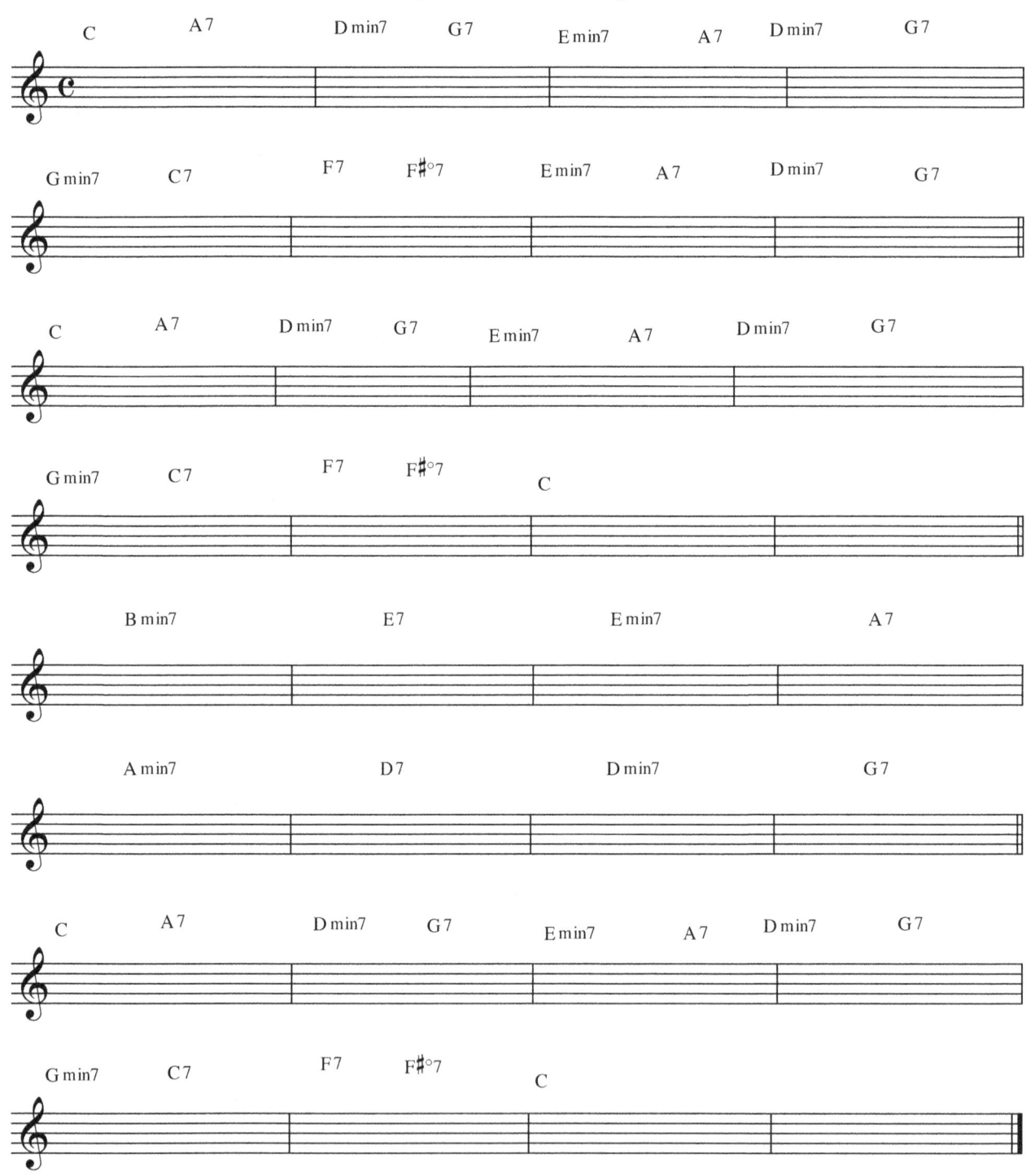

| C | A7 | D min7 | G7 | E min7 | A7 | D min7 | G7 |

| G min7 | C7 | F7 | F♯°7 | E min7 | A7 | D min7 | G7 |

| C | A7 | D min7 | G7 | E min7 | A7 | D min7 | G7 |

| G min7 | C7 | F7 | F♯°7 | C | | | |

| B min7 | E7 | E min7 | A7 |

| A min7 | D7 | D min7 | G7 |

| C | A7 | D min7 | G7 | E min7 | A7 | D min7 | G7 |

| G min7 | C7 | F7 | F♯°7 | C | | | |

Tune #1

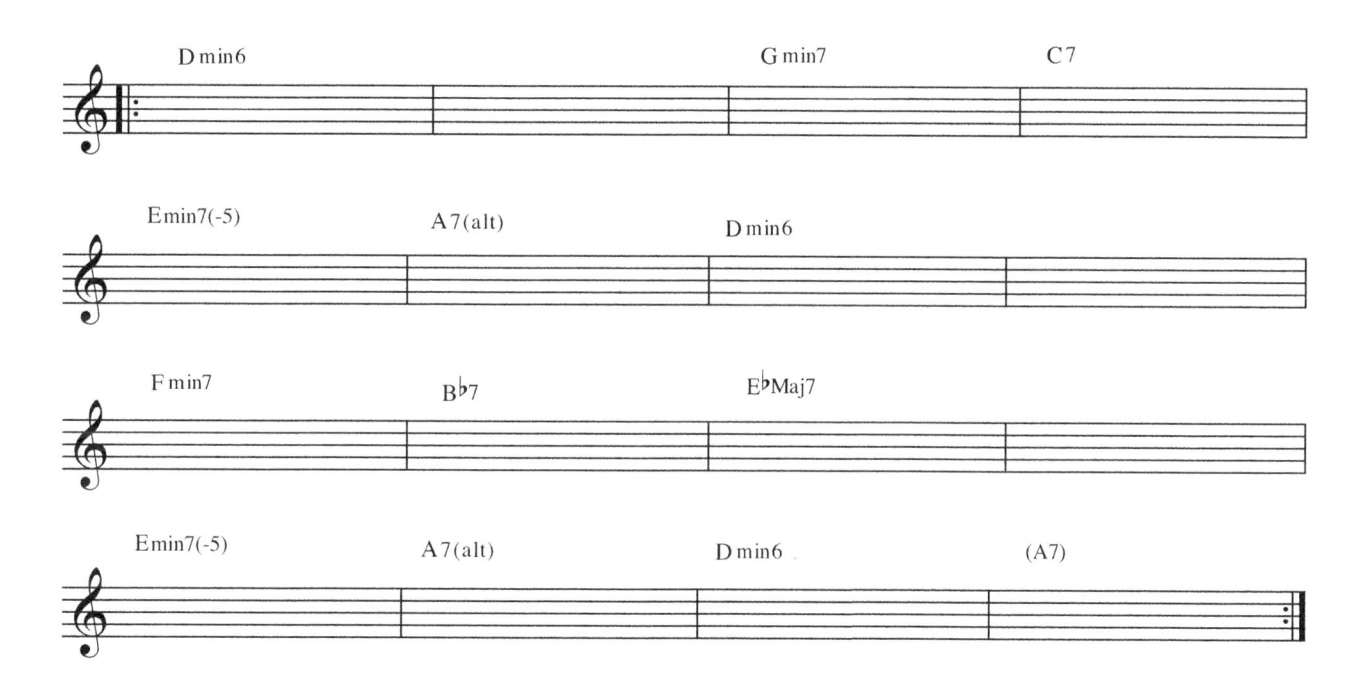

D min6		G min7	C7

E min7(-5)	A7(alt)	D min6	

F min7	B♭7	E♭Maj7	

E min7(-5)	A7(alt)	D min6	(A7)

Tune #2

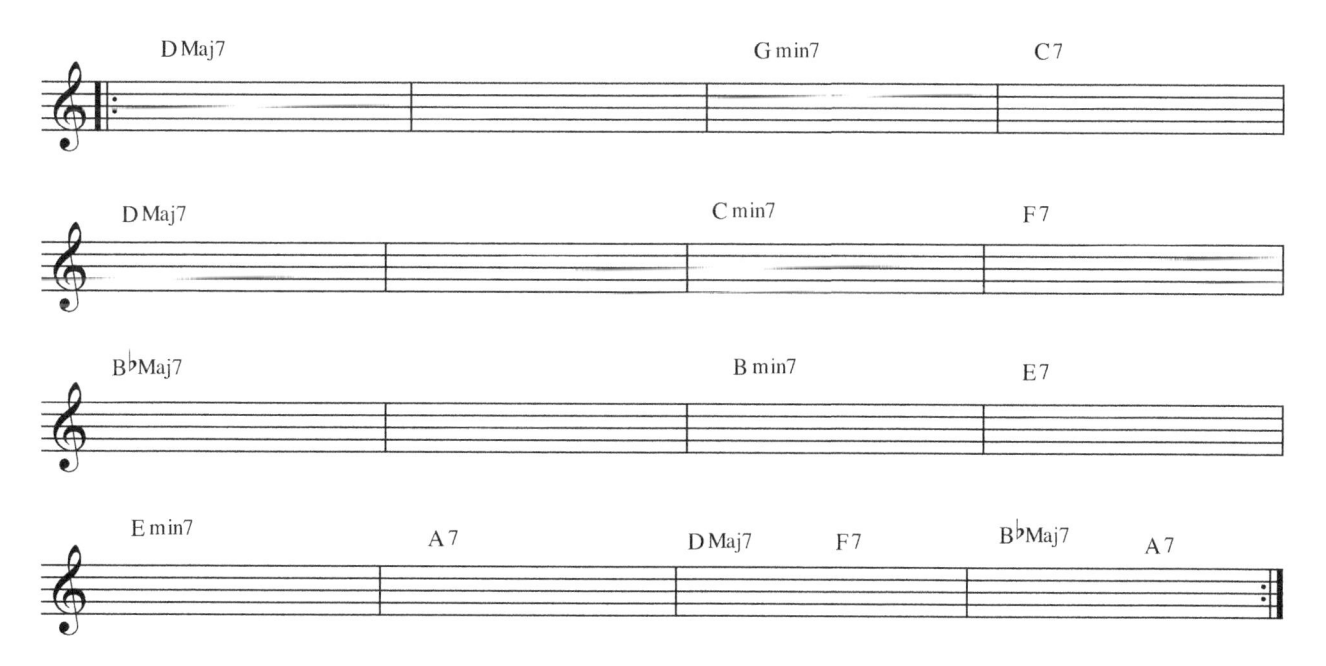

D Maj7		G min7	C7

D Maj7		C min7	F7

B♭Maj7		B min7	E7

E min7	A7	D Maj7　　F7	B♭Maj7　　A7

Blues in F

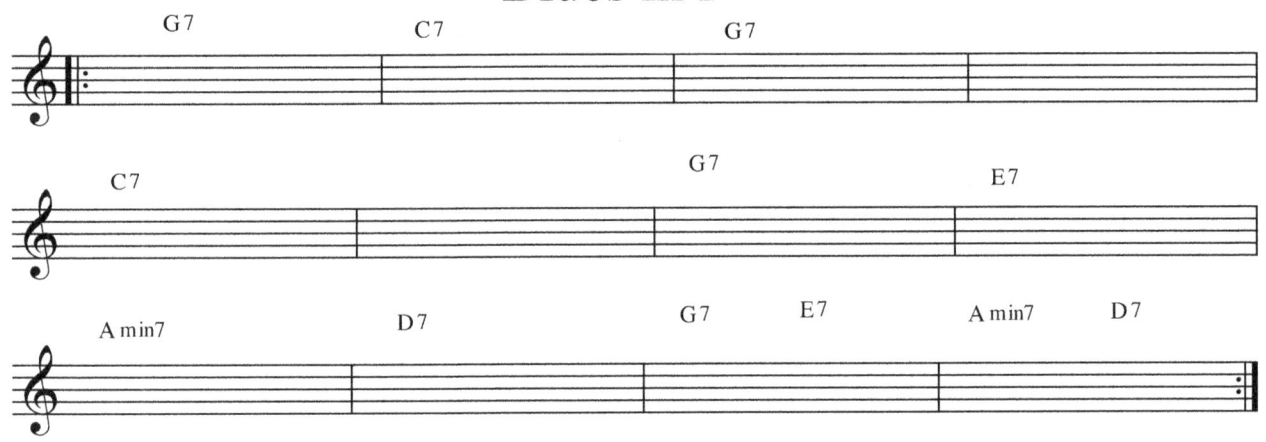

G7	C7	G7	

C7		G7	E7

Amin7	D7	G7　　E7	Amin7　　D7

Blues in Bb

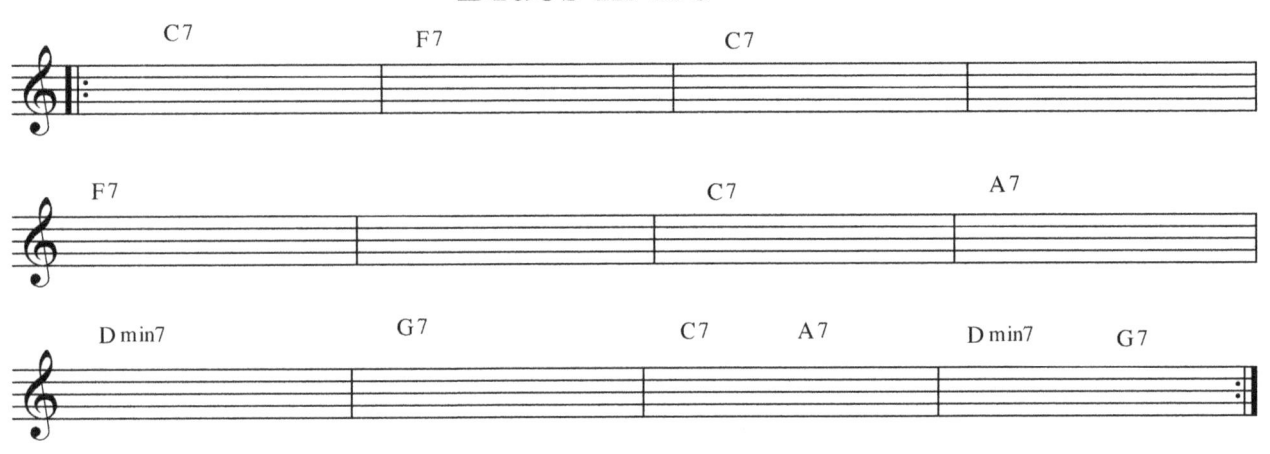

C7	F7	C7	

F7		C7	A7

Dmin7	G7	C7　　A7	Dmin7　　G7

Bird Blues

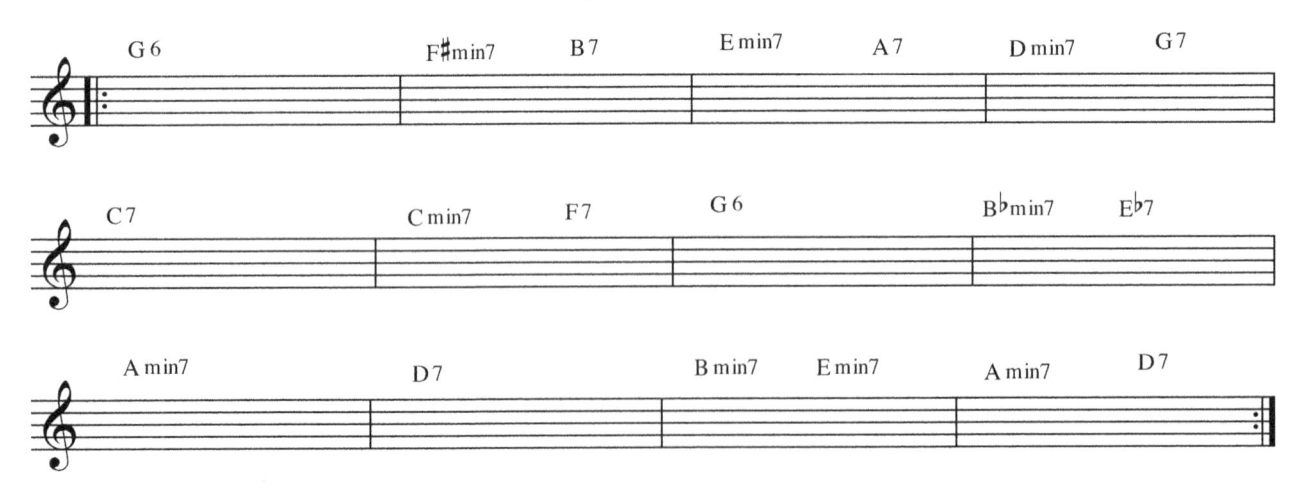

G6	F#min7　　B7	Emin7　　A7	Dmin7　　G7

C7	Cmin7　　F7	G6	Bbmin7　　Eb7

Amin7	D7	Bmin7　　Emin7	Amin7　　D7

21. Rhythm Exercises

Triplet Rhythms

Duple Rhythms

Combinations

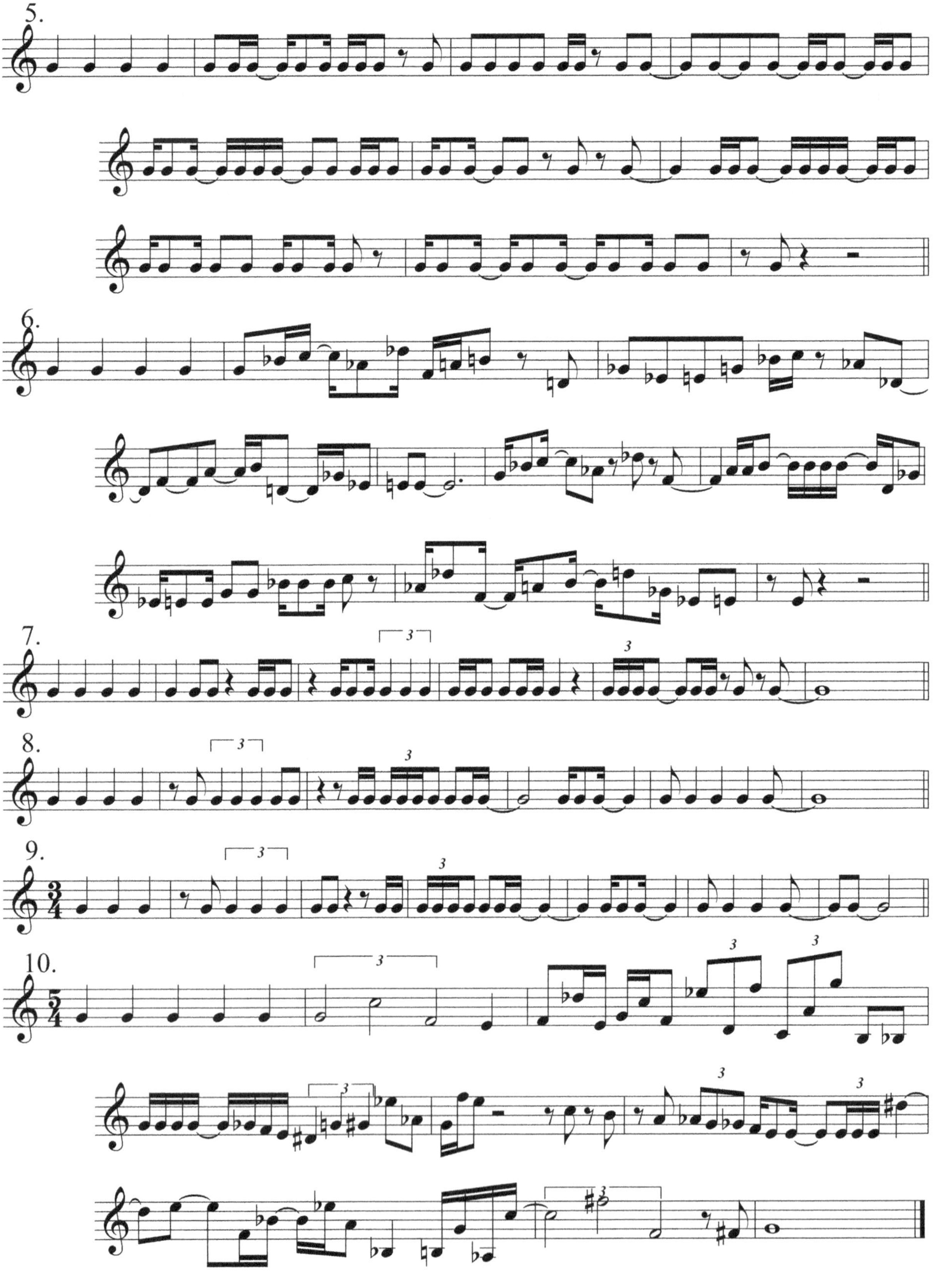
5.
6.
7.
8.
9.
10.

22. Scales

A Major

B Natural Minor

C Harmonic Minor

D Melodic Minor

15 Vocalises

Vocalise 1

Vocalise 2

Vocalise 3

Vocalise 4

Vocalise 5

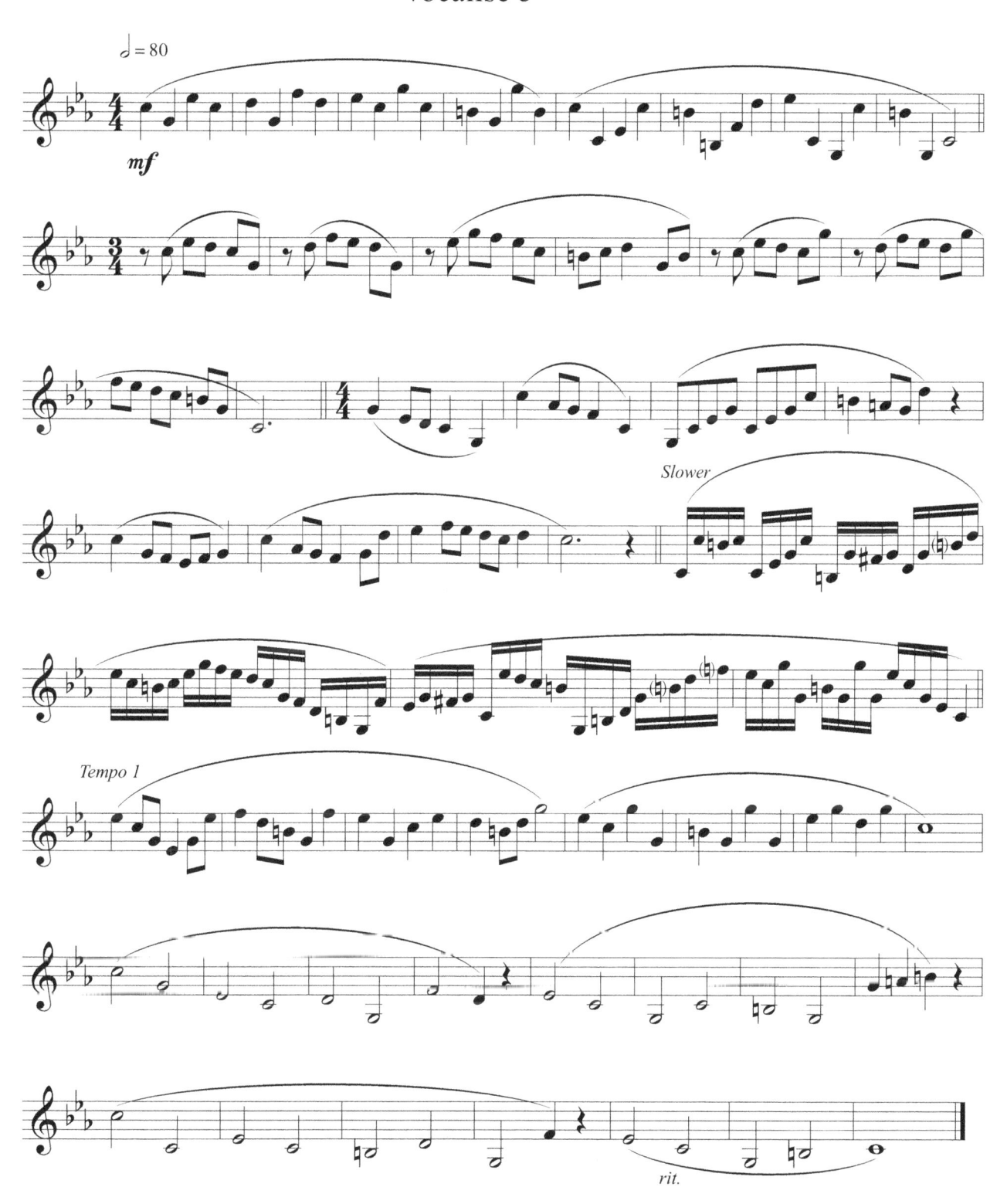

Vocalise 6

Vocalise 7

Vocalise 8

Vocalise 9

Vocalise 10

Vocalise 11

Vocalise 12

Vocalise 13

Vocalise 14

Vocalise 15

15 Rhythmical Etudes

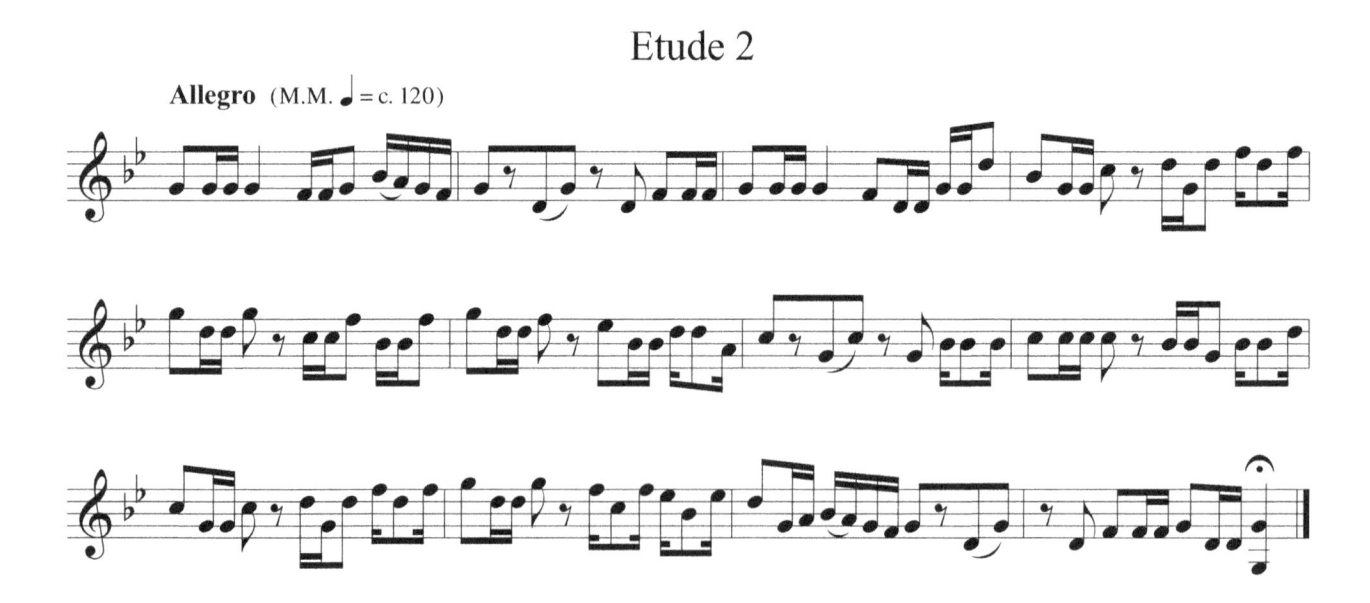

Etude 1

Moderato (♩ = c. 108)

Etude 2

Allegro (M.M. ♩ = c. 120)

Etude 3

Etude 4

Etude 5

Etude 6

Slowly, expressively

Etude 7

Etude 8

Playfully (M.M. ♩ = c. 120)

Etude 9

Etude 10

Etude 11

Etude 12

Etude 13

Etude 14

Etude 15

New from Randall Reyman...

Improvise Jazz Like the Pros...

IMPROVISE JAZZ LIKE THE PROS is the perfect instructional book for the intermediate-level jazz improviser who wants to step up their game. Ten advanced improvisational concepts used by professional jazz musicians are presented in concise and practical ways enabling the player to learn and incorporate them into their own solo improvisations. This book contains concepts such as the use of altered chord tones, chromaticism, pentatonics, tritone subs, triad pairs, and much more. Not intended for the beginning improvisor, IMPROVISE JAZZ LIKE THE PROS is an excellent text for the player who is ready to go to the next level and play like the pros!

Other trumpet and jazz books by Randall Reyman...

Technical Drills and Duets for the Jazz/Commercial Trumpet Player

The Fundamental Trumpet, Fundamental Exercises and Etudes for the Developing Trumpeter

Ultimate Chops, 16 Steps to Total Musicianship for Contemporary Instrumentalists

30 Progressive Jazz Duets for Trumpet

The *JAZZED ON JESUS* Fake Book, Traditional Hymns Re-harmonized for the Jazz/Commercial Musician

Get them all at...
www.RandallReyman.com

Made in the USA
Monee, IL
06 March 2020